ADHD In the Courtroom

ADHD in the Courtroom

Practicing Law with ADHD

By Michael L. Freeman

ADHD In the Courtroom
Copyright © 2026 by Michael L. Freeman

For permission requests, speaking inquiries, and bulk order purchase options, email michael@michaelfreemanlaw.com

This book is intended for informational and educational purposes only. It is not legal advice and does not create an attorney-client relationship. Laws, regulations, and interpretations change over time, and the author makes no representations or warranties as to the accuracy or completeness of the information contained herein. Readers should consult qualified legal counsel regarding their specific circumstances.

The views expressed in this book are solely those of the author and do not necessarily reflect the views of any employer, court, institution, or organization with which the author may be affiliated.

Any resemblance to actual persons or cases, living or deceased, is purely coincidental, except where otherwise noted.

ISBN: 979-8-234-00305-8
Published in the United States of America

Foreword

This book did not begin as a project about ADHD.

It began as an attempt to explain something that never quite fit the stories lawyers tell about competence, discipline, and failure. It began with the quiet recognition that there are lawyers who work harder than anyone around them and still feel perpetually behind. Lawyers who shine under pressure and struggle in silence afterward. Lawyers whose best work emerges in moments of urgency, while routine expectations quietly grind them down.

For a long time, those experiences were treated as personal shortcomings. Problems of organization. Problems of temperament. Problems of professionalism. The explanations were moral rather than structural, and the solutions were always the same: try harder, plan better, manage yourself more carefully.

That framing never matched reality.

Attention-Deficit/Hyperactivity Disorder is often spoken about as though it affects a small subset of people on the margins. In the general population, roughly 4.4 percent of adults carry an ADHD diagnosis. Even that number should matter. But in the legal profession, the prevalence is far higher. According to a 2016 study by the American Bar Association, approximately 12.5 percent of attorneys have been diagnosed with ADHD.

That is not an anomaly. It is a signal.

When a cognitive profile appears at nearly three times the rate in a profession compared to the population at large, the appropriate response is not suspicion or dismissal. It is curiosity. Law attracts certain minds. It rewards intensity, pattern recognition, verbal agility, tolerance for risk, and the ability to perform when the stakes are high. Those traits overlap meaningfully with how many ADHD brains operate, particularly under conditions of urgency and consequence.

The profession has benefited from that overlap for decades, often without realizing it.

At the same time, law was built on assumptions about time, attention, and emotional regulation that do not hold true for everyone who practices it. Calendars assume steady urgency. Administrative systems assume linear productivity. Professional norms assume emotional containment and predictable follow-through. These structures were not designed with neurological diversity in mind. They were inherited, normalized, and enforced long before ADHD was meaningfully understood.

The result is a quiet mismatch.

Many lawyers with ADHD succeed not because the system fits them, but because they learn to contort themselves around it. They compensate. They mask. They over-perform in visible arenas while absorbing invisible costs. They build workarounds without language for why those workarounds are necessary. From the outside, everything looks functional—until it doesn't.

This book is not an indictment of the legal profession, and it is not a manifesto. It does not argue that standards should be lowered or that responsibility should be abandoned. It argues for accuracy. It argues that performance cannot be evaluated honestly without understanding how different brains experience time, pressure, emotion, and initiation. It argues that many of the behaviors the system labels as failure make sense once context is restored.

Nothing in these pages suggests that lawyers with ADHD need to be fixed. There is nothing broken here. What is broken is the assumption that one cognitive style defines professionalism, competence, or reliability.

This book exists to name what has gone unnamed for too long. To give language to experiences that have been lived in isolation. To replace moral explanations with structural ones. To show that many lawyers who feel perpetually on the brink are not deficient, but operating under conditions that quietly tax them in ways the profession does not measure.

If you see yourself in these pages, the point is not to diagnose or excuse. It is to recognize. You cannot design a sustainable career around a problem you are not allowed to acknowledge. You cannot manage what you have been taught to interpret as a personal failing.

The legal profession is stronger because of the minds it attracts. It will only remain so if it learns to understand them.

That work begins here.

Author's Note

There's a kind of chaos that feels like home.

It's the quiet panic that sets in when everything is too still. It's the mind that wakes up at 2:00 a.m. with three unrelated thoughts, one brilliant, one irrelevant, and one that could probably get you disbarred if spoken out loud. It's the courtroom in your head that never adjourns.

For years, I thought I was simply wired wrong. That my brain was broken. That my career would eventually collapse under the weight of missed deadlines, forgotten filings, and the endless shame of knowing I could do great things, if only I could start.

When I was diagnosed with ADHD as an adult, it wasn't a relief. It was a reckoning. I finally had a name for the war I'd been fighting, but the diagnosis didn't come with a roadmap, just a label and a handful of pills that could focus my eyes but not my life.

Many disabilities are visible. They announce themselves to the world - a limp, a cane, a wheelchair, a tremor - and in doing so, they invite compassion, accommodation, even admiration for the strength it takes to endure. The world is built to recognize and, at least in theory, protect those disabilities. Society sees them and softens its tone.

ADHD is not such a disability.

It hides in plain sight. It does not draw pity; it draws judgment.

It's been mislabeled for decades — laziness, carelessness, apathy, immaturity. It's been treated as a moral failing dressed up as a diagnosis.

When people see ADHD, they don't see struggle; they see excuses.

And so the world responds with prescriptions and platitudes. It sits you down, hands you a bottle of Ritalin or Adderall, and tells you to behave. Then it leaves you alone — alone to fight the battle inside your head, alone to wrestle with the noise that never quiets and the silence that never lasts.

There are no ribbons for this. No ramps. No fundraisers.

Just the daily, invisible work of keeping your mind from running off without you.

And yet, that same restless mind — the one that's been called disordered — is often the same one that spots what others miss. The same one that connects ideas faster than most can follow. The same one that, under pressure, finds its rhythm and clarity in a courtroom, a crisis, or a closing argument.

ADHD isn't an excuse. It's an operating system.

The problem is, most of us never got the manual.

I learned that the hard way.

I was first diagnosed with ADHD during my first year of law school at Mississippi College School of Law. That diagnosis didn't come out of nowhere. I had known for years that my mind didn't move the way other people's did, even as a kid. I just didn't have language for it yet.

After a conversation with one of my professors, I was referred to a psychologist at Mississippi Baptist Hospital. She administered a battery of tests and confirmed what I had suspected but never named. Attention Deficit Hyperactivity Disorder.

The next step was supposed to be simple. She asked who my primary care physician was. I told her my doctor was in Knoxville, where I lived, not Jackson. She handed me a card instead.

The appointment was brief. The report was reviewed. A few questions were asked. I was prescribed Adderall, twenty milligrams, twice a day. One in the morning. One in the early afternoon. That, I was told, would take care of it.

In some ways, it did.

I remember the first time it kicked in. I cleaned my apartment from top to bottom. Organized my tools. Studied with a clarity I hadn't experienced before. Within weeks, I was dominating a Contracts class under the Socratic method, holding my own in extended back-and-forth with the professor in front of the room.

It felt like proof.

What it wasn't was a complete answer.

Years later, after practice, after trial work, after the pandemic, things began to shift. Focus became harder to summon. Writing became harder to start. Initiation friction crept back in, quieter this time, more confusing. The medication still worked in narrow ways, but it no longer touched the deeper mechanics of how my mind interacted with the work.

I saw psychiatrists. I read the books I was handed. None of them explained what I was actually experiencing. They focused on side effects. On dosage. On symptom control. They did not explain why the same brain that could perform cleanly under pressure could stall completely in silence.

That was the gap.

There are dozens of medications for ADHD. There is no single medication that addresses how executive function, time perception, emotional load, and environment collide inside a legal career. Pills can sharpen focus. They do not teach a system how to see you accurately.

I did not write this book to offer life hacks. I did not write it to promise mastery or control. I wrote it because ADHD does not stay static, and law practice does not forgive misunderstanding.

This book exists because what I needed did not exist when I went looking for it.

Introduction

This book does not require you to start at the beginning.

That is not a trick, and it is not a gimmick. It is an acknowledgment of how many lawyers with ADHD actually read. Some of you will move straight to the chapter that feels uncomfortably familiar. Some of you will skim, circle back, reread a section twice, skip another entirely, and then suddenly find yourself absorbed in a passage you did not expect to matter. That is not a failure of attention. It is how your mind gathers meaning.

You are allowed to read this book the same way you work: non-linear, pattern-driven, selective, and intuitive.

This is not a book about fixing yourself. It is not a productivity manual disguised as neuroscience. It is not a motivational sermon about grit, discipline, or "unlocking potential." And it is not an apology for having a brain that does not behave the way the profession assumes it should.

It is an attempt to describe what has already been happening.

If you have ADHD and you practice law, you already know the feeling of contradiction. You can perform at an extraordinarily high level in certain conditions and feel inexplicably stuck in others. You can think faster than the room during trial and then struggle later with tasks that appear simple on paper. You can be deeply committed to your clients and still find yourself fighting initiation, time, or emotional exhaustion in ways that feel disproportionate and hard to explain.

Most of the advice offered to lawyers with ADHD assumes the problem lives entirely inside the individual. Manage your symptoms. Improve your systems. Try harder to stay organized. Be more disciplined. That advice is not malicious, but it is incomplete. It treats neurological difference as a personal shortcoming rather than a variable interacting with an environment that was not designed with your brain in mind.

This book takes a different approach.

Instead of starting with solutions, it starts with recognition. Instead of asking how to override your wiring, it asks how your wiring actually works under real professional conditions. Instead of focusing only on outcomes, it pays attention to process, load, timing, and context—the things the legal system often ignores until something goes wrong.

You will notice that many chapters do not end with neat resolutions. That is intentional. The goal is not to give you a checklist that will magically resolve the friction you experience. The goal is to give language to patterns that are often misread or mislabeled, so you can stop interpreting them as personal failure.

Some chapters may feel like someone has been quietly watching your career. Others may feel less relevant. That is expected. ADHD is not a single experience, and neither is law practice. What matters is that you recognize yourself somewhere in these pages and realize that the things you have been struggling to name are neither imaginary nor unique.

This book also assumes something important about you: that you are competent.

It does not begin from the premise that lawyers with ADHD are broken, unreliable, or barely holding things together. In fact, many of the qualities that make you effective in practice, intensity, responsiveness, creativity, pattern recognition, emotional attunement, the ability to perform under pressure, are the same qualities that create strain when they are left unsupported or misunderstood. Strength and vulnerability are not opposites here. They are neighbors.

You will see that theme recur.

You will also see that this book does not pretend the profession is neutral. Law rewards certain cognitive styles and penalizes others, often without realizing it is doing so. Courtrooms, offices, calendars, billing systems, and disciplinary frameworks are built around assumptions about time, attention, and emotional regulation that do not hold true for everyone. When performance is evaluated without acknowledging those assumptions, behavior is easily misread.

That misreading has consequences.

Some of those consequences are professional. Some are personal. Many are quiet and cumulative rather than dramatic. This book is interested in those quiet accumulations, the invisible labor, the cognitive debt, the erosion of margin, because that is where most damage actually occurs.

You do not need to agree with everything you read here. You do not need to adopt every framework or resonate with every example. What matters is that you allow yourself to consider the possibility that your experience makes sense once the full picture is visible.

Much of what the legal profession believes it knows about ADHD was shaped during a period when public awareness expanded faster than clinical understanding. In the 1990s, attention to ADHD increased dramatically, but the first line of observation often occurred in classrooms rather than clinics. Teachers were frequently the ones who noticed students struggling with attention, impulse control, or classroom behavior and encouraged parents to seek evaluation.

In many cases, that evaluation occurred quickly and within a narrow framework. Pediatric visits often focused on observable behavior rather than deeper cognitive functioning, and medication became the most visible response. The result was not misconduct or bad faith, but a simplified public picture of a complex neurological condition.

That picture disproportionately emphasized hyperactive and disruptive behavior, most often in young boys. Over time, that emphasis shaped broader cultural assumptions. ADHD came to be associated with conduct issues children would outgrow, or with adults perceived as disorganized, undisciplined, or seeking shortcuts rather than support. What was lost in that translation was the full scope of the condition: inattentive presentation, executive function impairment, state-dependent performance, and the ways ADHD persists into adulthood without looking the way the stereotype predicts.

Once those early narratives hardened, they traveled. They moved from schools into workplaces, from pediatric offices into professional culture, and eventually into how entire fields—including law—came to interpret behavior. By the time ADHD reached the legal profession as a concept, it arrived filtered through oversimplified assumptions that no longer matched the clinical reality.

That legacy still shapes how ADHD is understood today.

As a result, when ADHD appears in adults, especially in professionals, it is often evaluated against a framework that was never designed to understand it. The legal profession inherited a model of ADHD built around childhood behavior, and it continues to apply that model to adult performance, where it no longer fits.

One more thing matters, and it is worth stating plainly.

You are not reading this book because you are failing at law. You are reading it because you are trying to understand why law sometimes feels harder than it should, even when you are doing it well. That question deserves a serious answer, not a platitude.

Take this book at your own pace. Skip around. Put it down and come back to it. Let certain chapters sit longer than others. This is not a test of attention or endurance.

When you are ready, the first chapter begins with a simple idea: that many lawyers with ADHD live with two versions of themselves operating at the same time, and that the tension between those versions has been misunderstood for far too long.

That is where the real conversation starts.

Contents

Part I

How the ADHD Lawyer's
Brain Actually Works

Chapter 1
The ADHD Brain
as a Split Screen
Why Output Alone Tells the Wrong Story

The courtroom was humming, not loudly, but insistently. It was the kind of vibration you feel more than hear, the low-grade tension that settles into a room where people's lives are being rearranged in real time. The Criminal Court for Davidson County, Tennessee. I was on my feet before I consciously decided to stand, objecting to a line of questioning that felt wrong in my bones.

"Objection, Your Honor."

She looked at me, calm and composed, the way judges do when they expect you to justify yourself. There was no impatience in her expression, no irritation. Just expectation.

"Give me a legal argument for that objection, Mr. Freeman."

That should have been easy. I knew the rule. I knew the rationale. I had made that objection before, in that courtroom and others like it. The law was there, ready, sitting just beneath the surface. But when her eyes settled on me, the words vanished.

My mind did not go blank. It exploded.

Thoughts scattered in every direction at once. I became aware of everything except the thing I needed. The lights overhead hummed a little too loudly. A juror shifted in her seat. Someone at the prosecution's table clicked a pen, once, twice. I caught the faint sweetness of the court reporter's perfume and wondered why my brain had decided that was worth noting.

At the same time, another part of me was already spiraling. I could feel it happening and could not stop it. I was thinking about how I must look standing there in silence. I wondered whether the judge thought I was unprepared. I questioned whether this was the moment people would later point to when they explained why I had never quite lived up to my potential. Somewhere in the middle of that storm, a completely unrelated thought intruded. Had I responded to that client's letter last week. The one asking me to come see him. Why was that in my head right now.

"Mr. Freeman?"

Her voice cut through the noise. I blinked and tried to anchor myself to the room. I reached for something usable. A phrase. A case name. A sentence that could get me out of the silence. What came out of my mouth was serviceable, but it was not what it should have been. It was half instinct and half improvisation. It broke the prosecutor's momentum enough to move on, but I knew I had missed the chance to land the point cleanly.

The objection was over. The trial moved forward. The jurors looked elsewhere. The judge turned her attention back to the witness. I sat down feeling exposed, as though something private had happened in public.

By the time court recessed for the day, my hands had not entirely steadied — though the moment itself had long since passed. I stepped outside the A. A. Birch Building in Nashville, Tenn. into that narrow stretch of concrete where the air always smells like exhaust, cigarettes, and the faint residue of stress. I lit one and let the smoke settle into my lungs, trying to slow my breathing. The city noise around me felt like a pulse I could not escape.

That was when the argument arrived. It came fully formed and cruelly perfect. Every rule. Every case. Every word I should have said lined up in order, as if my brain had been waiting for the worst possible moment to cooperate. I whispered it to myself, almost embarrassed by how obvious it was now. As if saying it aloud could somehow rewind the afternoon.

It was a simple issue. I had handled harder ones on less sleep with worse facts. I had more experience than the assistant district attorney asking the question. I had no business freezing the way I did. I knew exactly why it happened.

Attention Deficit Hyperactivity Disorder. ADHD. Four letters that had followed me since law school. Back then it was treated as a footnote. Something to manage. Something to keep an eye on. Take the medication. Make the lists. Build the systems. Stay organized. Control it. For a long time, I thought I had.

The Courtroom was the one place I never felt out of control. The chaos suited me. The pace matched the way my mind already worked. Trial was loud and fast and unpredictable, and in that environment, my brain made sense. I could move with the current instead of fighting it. I could think on my feet, connect ideas, read people, improvise. I was good there. Better than good. The trouble came when things slowed down.

Silence is dangerous for a brain like mine. Stillness invites interference. When a moment demands precision rather than momentum, clarity rather than instinct, the cracks start to show. That afternoon, standing in front of the Judge, I realized something I had spent years avoiding. ADHD does not disappear just because you know the law. It does not yield to experience. It waits for quiet and then takes advantage of it.

I replayed the moment again and again as the afternoon light reflected off the glass doors behind me. The objection. The pause. The panic. I told myself I would do better the next day. I would rest more. Prepare differently. Take my medication earlier. Fix it. I had been telling myself some version of that for years.

But I also knew this was not a fluke. It was a pattern.

I finished the cigarette and looked back at the courthouse steps. The wind caught my tie and lifted it slightly, as if urging me inside. I thought about the client sitting at the defense table, trusting me with his future. I thought about the jury, watching, evaluating. And I thought about the part of my mind that never stopped moving, even when everything around me demanded stillness.

That is the thing people misunderstand about ADHD. It is not an inability to focus. It is an inability to stop focusing on everything at once.

I had never been the lawyer who paced hallways before openings. Courtroom nerves were never part of my makeup. Standing in front of a jury felt natural, almost comfortable. It felt like home. I could take a tangled mess of facts and give it shape. I could tell a story that twelve strangers could follow and believe. When I spoke, I was not performing. I was connecting.

I have tried cases where two defendants sat side by side accused of the same conduct. Two lawyers. Same facts. Different outcomes. My client walked free while the other did not. It was never about ego. It was about clarity. I could see narrative lines others missed. I could rearrange the light and shadow until the truth came into focus.

That is why the freeze haunted me. It was not fear or inexperience. It was not even fatigue. It was something deeper and harder to explain. One moment I was ready for battle. The next, my own thoughts felt foreign.

It was the first time I noticed myself feeling out of sync in the courtroom. Not unprepared. Not disengaged. Just quieter than usual. A courthouse secretary approached me after a hearing and asked, without any pretense, whether I was feeling all right. The question caught me off guard, not because it was inappropriate, but because it confirmed something I had already been noticing in myself.

I had just finished a four-day jury trial and was, by any fair measure, exhausted. That part was expected. What was different was the way my energy had moved through the trial. Ordinarily, I lock in on day one and stay there. The rhythm of trial carries me. The longer it goes, the sharper I become. This time, the arc felt uneven.

The change did not come out of nowhere. After the pandemic, the Tennessee Supreme Court closed trial courts and designated criminal defense lawyers as essential workers. Our task was straightforward in concept and relentless in execution: move people out of jail as quickly and safely as possible. That meant bond reductions, negotiated resolutions, probation matters, and anything else that could reduce jail populations during a public health crisis.

The work itself was not complex, but it was constant. It required daily exposure to jails, closed environments, and a virus that was still poorly understood and widely feared. We accomplished a great deal. A significant number of people were released through lawful and appropriate means. It was meaningful work, but it was not trial work.

When jury trials resumed in 2022, I assumed I would feel rusty. Three years without a jury is a long gap for anyone who makes a living in that space. What surprised me was not rust, but variability.

On the first day of my first trial back, I felt slower than I expected. Not lost. Not unsure. Just not fully engaged yet. By the second day, the familiar edge returned. The third day was different again. My internal experience fluctuated in ways I had not encountered before. At times I was exactly where I needed to be. At other times, I felt as though I was operating on instinct and preparation alone, relying on systems I had built over years rather than the effortless intensity I was used to feeling.

Externally, the work did not suffer. The preparation was there. The advocacy was there. The constitutional obligations to my clients were met in full. Internally, though, I knew I was not operating at the level I expect of myself. That dissonance lingered.

The second trial confirmed it was not a permanent change. I was sharp. Focused. Fully engaged with the witnesses and the jury. Everything clicked the way it always had. After that, however, a pattern emerged. Every few hearings or trials, I would experience the same internal flattening. The work would get done. The outcomes were appropriate. But the feeling was wrong.

It was after one of those hearings that the secretary asked if I was all right. I remember standing there without an answer. The client had received the result we were seeking. There was nothing objectively wrong with the proceeding. Yet I knew I had not felt present in the way I normally do. That was the unsettling part.

Eventually, the fog lifted. As it often does with ADHD, the system recalibrated. The intensity returned. The hyperfocus that has always served me well in trial settings reasserted itself. When that happens, I know exactly where I am and what I am doing. I see angles quickly. I anticipate testimony. I can feel momentum shifting in the room.

What mattered during the in-between period was not how I felt, but what I did.

Even on days when my internal experience felt muted, my preparation did not change. If anything, it became more deliberate. I relied on process. I worked through witnesses methodically. I mapped anticipated questions and responses. I reviewed strengths and vulnerabilities with care. I trusted the systems I had built over years of practice.

That adherence to preparation is what carried me through. It is what allowed me to maintain consistency even when my internal state was less predictable. The work did not depend on inspiration. It depended on discipline.

Looking back, that period taught me something important. Performance is not a feeling. It is an outcome. And consistency is not about always feeling sharp. It is about building practices that hold when you do not.

That lesson stayed with me long after the fog cleared.

What people rarely see about ADHD is how invisible it is when things are going well. They see energy and confidence and quick thinking. They do not see the effort required to maintain that appearance. They do not see the internal negotiations, the constant compensation, the exhaustion that comes from managing a brain that does not regulate itself the way others do.

In the courtroom, adrenaline sharpens me. Urgency clears the noise. When the stakes are high, my mind locks in. But when that urgency drains away, the clarity goes with it. The drop is sudden and brutal. That day, the room went quiet and my brain scattered in search of stimulation.

This is not incompetence. It is chemistry.

ADHD is not a deficit of intelligence or preparation. It is a disorder of regulation. My brain does not filter well. It floods. Every stimulus arrives with the same intensity. Where other minds prioritize, mine improvises. And improvisation collapses when precision is required.

People think ADHD means distraction. What it actually means is hyperfocus misapplied. My mind did not wander because I did not care. It wandered because it was searching for the next spark. The next problem. The next fire, even if that fire existed only in my imagination.

That is the cruelty of it. You can be sharp one moment and lost the next. You can hold a room in the morning and struggle with silence by afternoon. It is not willpower. It is wiring.

Once I learned to name it, something shifted. This was not a personal failing. It was not laziness or weakness. It was an ADHD brain colliding with a system that demands calm, linear precision at exactly the moments my mind is least equipped to provide it.

I had never feared the courtroom. That day taught me to respect the silence. Because it is in the silence, not the storm, where ADHD does its quietest damage.

And that was when I finally admitted the truth. The real battle was never against the State of Tennessee. It was against my own mind, in a profession that punishes the way it works.

That moment in The Judge's courtroom stayed with me, not because it was dramatic, but because it refused to stay isolated. I wanted to believe it was a fluke, a bad beat in an otherwise solid record. What followed made that explanation impossible. As the courts reopened and jury trials returned after the long disruption of the pandemic, I began to notice the same internal disconnect appearing in quieter, less obvious ways.

Nothing was outwardly wrong. The work was done. The outcomes were acceptable. Yet the alignment I had relied on for years, the feeling that my mind would reliably lock in when it mattered, was no longer guaranteed. The split screen I had experienced in a single frozen moment had widened into a pattern, one that forced me to confront how ADHD operates not just in crisis, but over time, under sustained pressure, and in a profession that demands consistency even when the brain supplying it is anything but.

Chapter 2
ADHD and the Lawyer's Brain
Why This Is Neurology, Not Character

The air in a courtroom has a texture to it. You do not notice it if you are only there to resolve a traffic ticket or enter a plea and leave. But if you have stood there long enough, day after day, in front of twelve strangers and a judge who knows your habits better than you do, you start to feel it. You learn the way tension gathers. You learn how it hangs in the room before anyone speaks. You learn how it shifts when a witness hesitates or a juror leans back instead of forward.

Most lawyers hate that feeling. They talk about nerves, pressure, anxiety, the weight of responsibility. I never did. For me, that was the moment my brain finally woke up.

There is always a moment right before a trial begins. The prosecutor clears their throat. The bailiff adjusts their stance. The jurors settle into their seats, unaware that they are about to be asked to decide something that will alter another person's life forever. The room balances on an edge. For most lawyers, that moment feels like danger.

For me, it felt like oxygen.

People talk about ADHD as if it is a deficit, a disorder, a malfunction. The language always assumes something is missing. What they do not understand is that my mind was never off. It was idling. Waiting. Searching for the conditions that would allow it to do what it was built to do. The courtroom gave it those conditions.

Some people think best in silence. I think best when the stakes are real.

I learned early that my brain does not sit still inside my own head.

I don't mean distraction in the casual sense. I mean that even when I am doing the thing I am supposed to be doing, part of my attention is always elsewhere—monitoring, scanning, anticipating. It is as if my mind is running two processes at once: one handling the task in front of me, the other watching the room.

I noticed it most clearly in meetings.

I would be sitting at a conference table, listening carefully, taking notes, fully engaged. I could repeat back what had just been said without missing a word. And yet, at the same time, I was aware of everything else: who had stopped making eye contact, who seemed impatient, who was waiting to speak but hadn't yet found an opening. I tracked tone shifts. I tracked posture. I tracked when the energy in the room tightened or loosened.

None of this felt optional. It simply happened.

Later, when someone would ask a question about the substance of the discussion, I answered easily. When someone asked how the room "felt," I answered that too. What surprised me was that other people seemed to treat these as separate skills. For me, they were inseparable. I could not turn one off without losing the other.

This became more pronounced in court.

While arguing a motion, I am not only thinking about the legal standard. I am listening for the judge's breathing, watching for impatience, sensing when an interruption is coming before it arrives. I adjust mid-sentence, sometimes without realizing I have done so. I shorten an argument instinctively. I abandon a point I had planned to make because the room no longer supports it.

Afterward, colleagues sometimes ask how I knew to pivot when I did. I usually don't have a satisfying answer. I didn't decide. I responded.

That responsiveness comes at a cost.

Because the same brain that absorbs the room so completely also struggles with quiet, unstructured space. Sitting alone in my office, staring at a file that does not speak back, does not move, does not react, my mind looks for signals. When none arrive, attention drifts. Not because I don't care, but because the environment is silent in a way my brain does not know how to prioritize.

What took me years to understand is that this pattern has its own internal logic.

The ADHD brain is not broken. It is tuned. It is exquisitely sensitive to input—especially human input. It excels where feedback is immediate and information is dynamic. It struggles where feedback is delayed and significance must be imagined rather than felt.

That same sensitivity that makes me effective in live environments means my brain is always working harder than it appears. It is processing more data, more variables, more signals than the task technically requires. And when the task offers nothing back, the system stalls.

For a long time, I assumed this meant something was wrong with my discipline.

I tried to force stillness. I tried to simplify my thinking. I tried to "just focus." None of that worked, because it misunderstood the problem. The issue was not effort. It was architecture. My brain was designed to operate in interaction, not isolation.

Once I understood that, the contradictions in my performance began to make sense.

I wasn't unreliable. I was state-dependent.

And the lawyer's brain I was told I was supposed to have—the linear, steady, uniform one—was never the brain I was working with in the first place.

What I did not understand then was that this wasn't intuition running hot — it was executive function carrying two loads at once, handling the substance of the work while compensating for processes my brain does not automate.

The Rush

Trial is not just a test of legal skill. It is a sensory environment. The shuffle of the jury box. The hum of the lights overhead. The posture of a witness who thinks they are in control. The subtle shift in a judge's expression when an argument lands or misses. All of it creates a kind of electrical current that snaps my attention into place.

While other people build focus through routine and discipline, mine arrives through intensity. When the stakes rise, my clarity sharpens. When they fall, it evaporates. That is the paradox of an ADHD brain. It can deliver extraordinary performance under pressure and near paralysis in the ordinary.

I remember sitting through jury selection in a murder case, watching the prosecutor beside me shuffle papers and reorganize notes. He glanced over at me and saw nothing in front of me. No yellow pad. No outline. No stack of exhibits. He assumed I was unprepared. What he could not see was that my mind was already moving ahead of the room. I was tracking juror reactions, noting who leaned in and who crossed their arms, listening for language patterns in answers that hinted at bias or hesitation. My attention was split between the external performance and an internal mapping process that was running faster than anything I could have written down.

Trial did not feel like pressure. It felt like alignment.

The Storm Brain

Outside the courtroom, things were never that simple.

People assume that if someone can dismantle a detective on cross-examination, they should be able to remember where they left their keys. Or show up on time for a meeting. Or respond to a basic email without rewriting it a dozen times. That assumption misses the point entirely.

ADHD is not a universal impairment. It is a state-dependent brain. Context dictates competence.

Give me a constitutional issue buried beneath layers of procedural noise and I will take it apart piece by piece. Ask me to remember an appointment scheduled three days from now and the odds are not in our favor.

I have prepared for trial overnight, pulling together case law, forensic reports, jail calls, and witness statements into a coherent strategy with absolute clarity. Then I have walked out the door the next morning without my phone or the file I needed most. To someone watching from the outside, that looks like carelessness. From the inside, it feels like living with a mind that burns hot in one direction while leaving everything else in shadow.

The problem is not that I do not care. The problem is that I care intensely and unevenly. Hyperfocus can be a gift in the courtroom and a liability everywhere else. It allows me to see patterns others miss and connections that do not announce themselves. It also makes it easy to disappear down a rabbit hole that has no bearing on what actually needs to be done that day.

The storm is not chaos. It is power without consistent control.

Chemistry, Not Character

There is a loop inside the ADHD brain driven by chemistry rather than intention. Dopamine and norepinephrine regulate motivation, attention, and reward. In an ADHD brain, those systems do not respond reliably to importance or obligation. They respond to urgency, novelty, conflict, and challenge.

That is not a metaphor. It is structural. It is anatomical.

Trial law happens to deliver those elements in abundance. Cross-examination creates immediate feedback. A jury's silence carries weight. Objections land or fail in real time. The brain lights up because the environment demands it.

In that sense, the courtroom functions like medication. It supplies stimulation externally that other people generate internally. The focus feels effortless because it is chemically supported by the situation itself.

But there is always a crash.

After a trial ends, the stimulation drops. The urgency disappears. The chemistry shifts. What felt effortless suddenly becomes exhausting. While others celebrate or decompress, the silence feels abrasive. The mind that just ran at full capacity is left searching for the next source of alignment.

I remember walking out of a courtroom after a hard-fought acquittal. The defendant's family was crying and hugging. The prosecutor avoided eye contact. The judge nodded quietly and moved on to the next case. Everyone in the room felt the weight of what had just happened.

Outside, in the heat of the afternoon, the quiet felt wrong. The fire was gone. Winning did not bring peace. It brought absence.

The storm had aligned my mind. The aftermath left it restless.

The Discipline Myth

People without ADHD talk about discipline as if it were a simple choice. They assume that focus is something you apply evenly across tasks if you care enough. When they see moments of extraordinary concentration, they assume that same effort could be summoned at will.

What they do not see is the cost.

They do not see the friction required to start tasks that offer no stimulation. They do not see the internal bargaining, the compensating, the energy spent simply trying to begin. What looks like inconsistency from the outside often reflects neurological exhaustion on the inside.

ADHD is not an attention deficit. It is an attention regulation disorder. I do not choose what captures my focus. I respond to what activates it. Some days, I can draft a closing argument in a single sitting. Other days, sending a short email feels insurmountable.

Discipline has never been absent. The expectation that discipline alone should override neurology has been the real failure.

What people label laziness is often effort no one bothered to measure.

The Edge and the Cost

There is a reason ADHD brains thrive under pressure. They are tuned for vigilance. They scan for threat and opportunity. They react quickly and adapt faster. In a different context, that wiring would be an asset without apology.

Instead, we operate in systems built around schedules, forms, and incremental tasks. The battlefield has been replaced by inboxes and calendar alerts. The danger is no longer immediate, but the brain does not adjust easily to that shift.

For a long time, I assumed the problem was me. That my mind was broken or deficient. It took years to understand that it was not broken. It was miscast.

My brain was not built for fluorescent lights and administrative routines. It was built for conflict, stakes, and decision-making under pressure. That realization did not solve everything, but it reframed the problem.

The tragedy is not the wiring. The tragedy is a profession that benefits from it in moments of crisis and punishes it in moments of quiet.

Once I understood that, the rest of this book began to make sense. The struggles were not isolated failures. They were predictable outcomes of a brain designed for intensity operating in a system that demands consistency without accommodation.

My brain was never broken. It was built for a different kind of fight.

The ADHD brain does not regulate attention evenly across contexts. Attention is not "on" or "off," but contingent. Factors such as urgency, novelty, emotional salience, and immediacy influence whether executive function engages fully, partially, or not at all. This variability is not a reflection of motivation or intelligence. It reflects how the brain allocates cognitive resources in response to stimulation.

Tasks that generate sufficient activation tend to organize attention automatically. Tasks that do not require the brain to self-generate structure, urgency, and prioritization. When that internal generation fails, performance degrades—not because the individual is unwilling or incapable, but because the regulatory mechanism did not engage.

This state-dependent regulation explains why effort does not produce consistent output and why planning alone is often insufficient. Without adequate activation, intention stalls. With it, performance can become sharply focused and sustained.

Masking in Legal Practice

There is a version of me that walks into court, and there is a version of me that exists everywhere else. The version in court is calm, articulate, prepared, and responsive. He knows where to stand, when to speak, and how to project certainty even when the ground underneath is shifting. Judges see him. Jurors trust him. Colleagues assume he is steady.

What they do not see is the work required to maintain that appearance.

Masking is the process by which a person with ADHD suppresses natural cognitive patterns in order to meet external expectations. In the legal profession, masking is not optional. The system rewards polish, responsiveness, and emotional containment. Distraction, hesitation, and inconsistency are treated not as neurological variance but as character flaws. So lawyers with ADHD learn early to hide the effort.

Masking begins before the work does. It starts with rehearsing conversations, anticipating objections that may never come, and double checking tone in emails that should have taken thirty seconds to send. It continues through hearings where attention is split between the substance of the argument and the performance of competence. It ends late at night, long after the file is closed, when the adrenaline fades and the cost shows up as exhaustion.

From the outside, masking looks like professionalism. Inside, it feels like running a background program that never shuts off.

The danger is not that masking fails immediately. The danger is that it works well enough to become invisible. Judges see a lawyer who appears organized. Clients see someone who seems attentive. Colleagues see a person who gets things done. Over time, that external feedback reinforces the idea that the internal cost is irrelevant.

It is not.

Masking consumes executive function. Every ounce of energy spent maintaining the appearance of control is energy not available for drafting, planning, or recovery. This is why many lawyers with ADHD perform best under pressure and worst in routine settings. Trial provides structure, urgency, and novelty. Masking aligns with the task. Administrative work provides none of those things, and the cognitive load becomes unsustainable.

This creates a dangerous illusion. Because the lawyer can perform at a high level in court, the system assumes the same level of performance is available everywhere else. When it is not, the explanation defaults to laziness, disorganization, or lack of discipline. The reality is simpler and harder to accept. The brain is already working harder than it appears.

Masking also distorts self perception. When success depends on constant self correction, it becomes difficult to trust one's own competence. Wins feel fragile. Mistakes feel catastrophic. The internal narrative shifts from confidence to vigilance. That vigilance is exhausting, and exhaustion is cumulative.

Over time, masking stops being a strategy and becomes a liability. The lawyer still looks functional, but the margin for error disappears. Small disruptions carry outsized consequences. Deadlines slip. Communication suffers. Not because the lawyer stopped caring, but because there is nothing left to give.

This is why so many high performing lawyers with ADHD reach a breaking point that seems to come out of nowhere. It is not sudden. It is deferred.

Understanding masking does not excuse errors. It explains why they cluster. It explains why warning signs are missed. It explains why competence can coexist with collapse.

The legal profession rewards those who can maintain the mask. It rarely asks what the mask costs.

Executive Function Failure Is Not Incompetence

One of the most damaging misunderstandings about ADHD in the legal profession is the assumption that when something goes wrong, the failure must be intellectual. Missed deadlines are treated as carelessness. Disorganization is treated as sloppiness. Delayed responses are treated as disrespect. The underlying belief is that if a lawyer is smart enough to understand the law, then they should be able to manage the mechanics of practicing it.

That belief is wrong.

ADHD is not a deficit of intelligence. It is a disorder of executive function. Executive function governs the brain's ability to initiate tasks, sequence steps, hold information in working memory, regulate attention, estimate time, and shift between tasks appropriately. These are not peripheral skills in law. They are the job.

When executive function falters, it does not look like ignorance. It looks like inconsistency. A lawyer can deliver a precise oral argument in the morning and forget to send a confirming email in the afternoon. They can dismantle an expert witness on cross examination and then miss a routine filing deadline. They can understand exactly what needs to be done and still fail to start it.

This is the part that confuses people who do not live inside an ADHD brain. The knowledge is there. The intent is there. The ability is there. The execution is not.

Executive function failure is state dependent. It fluctuates with stress, sleep, stimulation, emotional load, and environmental demands. That means performance is not stable across contexts. A lawyer may function at an elite level in court, where urgency and structure activate the brain, and struggle profoundly with administrative tasks that offer no immediate consequence or feedback.

The legal system is built on the assumption that competence is consistent. ADHD exposes the flaw in that assumption.

What makes this particularly dangerous is that executive function failure is invisible when things are going well. A lawyer who prepares meticulously for trial is assumed to be capable of the same level of organization everywhere else. When that consistency breaks down, the explanation defaults to character. Not effort. Not load. Not neurology.

Character.

This is how executive function impairment becomes moralized.

From the inside, the experience is maddening. You know what needs to be done. You may even feel the urgency. But the signal that allows action to begin does not fire. The task remains abstract. Time collapses. What should take thirty minutes stretches into avoidance, not because of fear, but because the brain cannot assemble the starting sequence.

This is not procrastination in the casual sense. It is not choosing rest over work. It is a breakdown in task initiation and regulation. Telling yourself to try harder does not fix it. Punishing yourself for it makes it worse.

Executive function failure also explains why many lawyers with ADHD over prepare. When you cannot rely on internal sequencing, you compensate with repetition, redundancy, and exhaustive preparation. You write more notes than necessary. You review the file more times than others. You build systems to make up for what your brain will not do automatically.

That compensation works until it does not.

When the load exceeds the system, failure appears sudden to outsiders. It is not sudden. It is cumulative.

Understanding executive function failure reframes the problem. It shifts the question from "Why didn't you do this?" to "What conditions prevented execution?" That shift is not an excuse. It is a prerequisite for designing practices, accommodations, and safeguards that prevent predictable breakdowns.

Law does not fail lawyers with ADHD because it demands intelligence. It fails them because it assumes execution follows knowledge automatically.

It does not.

When executive function fails quietly, it looks like inconsistency. When it fails under pressure, it looks like paralysis. The same neurological bottleneck that makes sequencing difficult also makes starting feel impossible once the stakes rise and the margin shrinks. That is when knowledge stops mattering. That is when intention becomes irrelevant. And that is when the lawyer is left staring at work they fully understand but cannot initiate. What follows is not laziness or avoidance. It is task paralysis, and it is where the consequences of an unmanaged ADHD brain become impossible to ignore.

Chapter 3
State-Dependent Performance:
Why the Same Lawyer Can Be Elite One Day & Unreliable the Next

The legal profession is built on an assumption it rarely names: that performance is stable.

Once a lawyer demonstrates competence, that competence is expected to travel with them—to every courtroom, every office, every deadline, every administrative task, regardless of conditions. Preparation is presumed to equal availability. Skill is presumed to be accessible on demand. Excellence, once proven, is treated as portable.

For many lawyers, that assumption holds well enough to go unexamined.

For lawyers with ADHD, it does not.

What this book calls state-dependent performance is not a theory. It is an observable pattern. The same lawyer can perform at an extraordinarily high level in one context and struggle to initiate or sustain work in another, even when the stakes are identical. The difference is not intelligence. It is not commitment. It is not professionalism. It is state.

Performance depends on the neurological conditions present at the moment the work is required.

That idea alone explains more professional confusion, shame, and misinterpretation than almost anything else discussed in this book.

The ADHD brain does not operate on a flat plane. It operates in peaks and valleys shaped by urgency, stimulation, clarity, emotional load, novelty, and consequence. When those variables align, performance can be exceptional—sometimes startlingly so. When they do not, performance can degrade in ways that feel disproportionate and inexplicable, both to the lawyer and to everyone watching.

From the outside, this looks like inconsistency.

From the inside, it feels like betrayal.

The lawyer knows they can do the work. They have done it before. They may have done it brilliantly. That memory makes later difficulty feel personal. If I could do it then, why can't I do it now? The question carries an accusation embedded in it, even when no one else voices one.

The profession rarely supplies an alternative explanation.

Instead, it defaults to a moral one.

When performance fluctuates, the legal system looks for internal causes. Motivation. Discipline. Focus. Prioritization. Values. When those explanations fail to account for the pattern, the conclusion hardens: something must be wrong with the lawyer.

State-dependent performance offers a different framework.

It says that the problem is not unreliability, but conditional access. The lawyer's abilities are real, but they are not equally available across all environments and moments. Certain states unlock them. Others obstruct them. The difference is not effort alone. It is how the brain is being asked to operate at that time.

This is easiest to see in the courtroom.

Court supplies structure automatically. There is a schedule. There are rules. There is an audience. There are immediate consequences. There is emotional charge. Time is compressed. Stakes are visible. Feedback is instant. The brain does not have to imagine urgency—it is sitting in the room.

For many lawyers with ADHD, this environment brings clarity. Focus sharpens. Words come easily. Decisions are made quickly. Pattern recognition accelerates. The lawyer feels present and effective. This is often where they are at their best.

The same lawyer may then return to the office and struggle with tasks that appear objectively easier. Drafting. Reviewing. Organizing. Responding. Planning. The work is familiar. The law is settled. The stakes are still real. Yet initiation stalls. Attention slips. Time blurs.

The profession reads this as contradiction.

It is not. It is continuity.

The courtroom provides external scaffolding the ADHD brain does not reliably generate on its own. When that scaffolding disappears, the same brain is asked to supply internally what was previously supplied externally. Sometimes it can. Often it cannot. The difference is not character. It is state.

This distinction matters because it reframes what "inconsistency" actually means.

Inconsistency does not always reflect unreliability. Sometimes it reflects variability in neurological access. The lawyer is the same. The demands are the same. The environment is not.

The legal profession struggles with this idea because it collides with a deeply ingrained belief: that competence should be self-contained. A good lawyer should be able to perform anywhere, under any conditions, without accommodation. The moment that belief is challenged, the profession becomes uncomfortable. If competence is contextual, then environment matters. If environment matters, then systems are implicated. And once systems are implicated, responsibility is no longer purely personal.

That discomfort shows up later as resistance.

State-dependent performance also explains why traditional advice often fails lawyers with ADHD. Time management systems. Organizational tools. Productivity frameworks. These tools assume a brain that can initiate action based on abstract future consequence. They assume that knowing something matters is enough to make it actionable.

For an ADHD brain, knowledge alone rarely moves behavior.

Action requires activation. Activation requires state.

This is why motivation cannot be summoned at will. This is why discipline does not reliably overcome friction. This is why a lawyer can care deeply about a case and still struggle to begin work on it until pressure spikes. The brain is not refusing to cooperate. It is waiting for conditions it recognizes as real.

Urgency is one of those conditions.

Urgency collapses time. It converts future consequence into present demand. When urgency arrives, performance often follows. This is not laziness. It is neurology. The ADHD brain responds more reliably to immediate consequence than to distant abstraction.

The profession treats this as a flaw.

In reality, it is a different operating system.

State-dependent performance also explains why praise and punishment often miss the mark. When a lawyer performs well under pressure, the system attributes success to competence. When the same lawyer struggles later, the system attributes difficulty to neglect. Both conclusions ignore state.

The lawyer is rewarded and disciplined as though the underlying variable were fixed.

It is not.

This misreading creates a specific kind of harm. The lawyer begins to doubt their own perceptions. They remember moments of clarity and excellence and assume those moments represent the "real" version of themselves. Everything else becomes deviation. When difficulty arises, they interpret it as backsliding, weakness, or decline.

Over time, this internal narrative becomes corrosive.

Instead of asking what conditions made performance possible, the lawyer asks what is wrong with them. They push harder in states where pushing is least effective. They add hours instead of structure. They absorb shame instead of examining design.

The system reinforces this pattern by praising sacrifice and punishing friction.

State-dependent performance also exposes why disclosure is so fraught. When a lawyer tries to explain that they perform differently in different contexts, the explanation often sounds evasive to people who assume uniformity. If performance should be stable, then variability sounds like excuse. Without a shared framework, explanation fails.

That failure is not rhetorical. It is structural.

This chapter matters because it changes how everything that follows should be read.

Task paralysis is not procrastination. It is failed activation in a low-urgency state.

Time blindness is not carelessness. It is distorted temporal perception when future consequence lacks emotional weight.

Overcommitment is not irresponsibility. It is optimism generated during high-activation states that does not survive later conditions.

The activation barrier is not resistance to work. It is the cost of transitioning between incompatible states.

Disciplinary misinterpretation is not simply harshness. It is evaluation based on outcomes without regard to conditions.

Once state-dependent performance is understood, these patterns stop looking random.

They become predictable.

This does not eliminate responsibility. It clarifies it.

Responsibility in a state-dependent framework is not about forcing uniform output. It is about designing conditions that allow capacity to surface reliably. It is about recognizing where performance is strongest and structuring practice accordingly. It is about reducing friction where friction predictably undermines initiation. It is about externalizing scaffolding instead of demanding it appear internally.

The legal profession rarely teaches this because it assumes everyone has the same internal regulators. That assumption is false. But it persists because it simplifies evaluation. Uniform standards are easier to enforce than contextual ones.

Ease, however, is not accuracy.

This chapter is not asking the profession to abandon standards. It is asking it to understand what standards are actually measuring. When performance is treated as a moral constant instead of a contextual outcome, both lawyers and systems misread what is happening.

State-dependent performance is the through-line of this book because it explains the central paradox many ADHD lawyers live with: being highly capable and persistently vulnerable at the same time.

That paradox is not a contradiction. It is a signal.

And once it is recognized as such, the next chapters become unavoidable.

Because if performance depends on state, then time, urgency, emotional load, environment, and structure are no longer side issues.

They are the work.

Chapter 4
ADHD is a Disability
(Not a Sin)
Why Moral Judgment Has No Place in Professional Evaluation

When the judge interrupted me in Chapter 1, the problem was not the objection, or even the ruling. It was the assumption—shared by everyone in that courtroom, including me—that my mind would remain linear under interruption. ADHD does not fail gradually in moments like that; it collapses. Working memory overloads, sequencing disintegrates, and time ceases to behave normally. What looked, from the outside, like hesitation or uncertainty was in fact a predictable shutdown of executive control under stress. I did not freeze because I was unprepared or unsure of the law. I froze because my cognitive operating system encountered a condition it is uniquely bad at surviving without warning.

There is a moment that comes for almost every lawyer who lives with ADHD, whether they name it or not. It usually arrives quietly, after the third or fourth time a routine task slips through the cracks. A deadline that should have been easy. A follow-up that somehow never happened. A billing entry that made perfect sense in real time and vanished once the moment passed.

The instinct, especially for lawyers, is to turn inward. To tighten the lens around personal responsibility. To ask what you should have done differently. Taken your medication more consistently. Built better systems. Tried harder. Paid closer attention. Not let the ADHD win.

All of that matters. None of it is enough.

Because there is another force at work here, one the legal profession rarely acknowledges. The problem is not confined to the individual lawyer's brain. It is embedded in the way the profession evaluates competence, assigns blame, and interprets struggle.

The legal system has a habit of moralizing what it does not understand.

Disability Law & the Legal Profession's Blind Spot

Attention Deficit Hyperactivity Disorder is recognized as a disability under the Americans with Disabilities Act. That is not a controversial statement. Federal law has long acknowledged that ADHD can substantially limit major life activities, including concentrating, organizing, planning, working, and thinking. These are not abstract concepts. They are the daily building blocks of legal practice.

The profession knows this in theory. In practice, it often behaves as if the diagnosis stops at the courthouse door.

Lawyers are evaluated through outcomes. Deadlines met or missed. Calls returned or not. Files advanced or stalled. Those outcomes are then read backward into character assessments. Diligent or neglectful. Responsible or careless. Professional or not.

What rarely enters the analysis is whether the behavior in question is tied to a recognized disability that directly affects executive function. The system sees the symptom and assumes intent. It sees inconsistency and assumes indifference. It sees struggle and assigns blame.

This is not because lawyers are cruel. It is because the profession has trained itself to believe that competence is uniform and portable. That a good lawyer should perform the same way in every room, under every condition, at every hour of the day. That belief is deeply ingrained. It is also wrong.

Executive Function Is Not a Character Trait

Executive function is not willpower. It is not discipline. It is not professionalism in the moral sense. It is a set of cognitive processes governed by neurobiology. Working memory. Task initiation. Time perception. Emotional regulation. Cognitive flexibility.

When those processes are impaired, the impairment does not announce itself politely. It shows up as friction. Delay. Avoidance. Overwhelm. Missed transitions. The work gets done, just not always in the order or on the timeline the profession expects.

Outside of law, this distinction is better understood. In medicine, performance issues are often evaluated through an impairment lens before discipline is imposed. In education, behavior is assessed to determine whether it is a manifestation of disability. In federal employment, agencies are required to engage in an interactive process when disability may be affecting performance.

Law, by contrast, tends to skip that step. It moves quickly from observation to judgment. The missed deadline becomes evidence of neglect. The disorganized file becomes evidence of incompetence. The delayed response becomes evidence of disregard.

The disability never makes it into the record unless the lawyer forces it there.

Why This Mislabeling Matters

This is not an abstract concern. The consequences are real. When disability-driven behavior is misinterpreted as misconduct, the system responds with punishment rather than accommodation. Lawyers internalize that response. They try harder. They hide symptoms. They overcompensate. They work longer hours under worse conditions. They avoid disclosure because they fear being seen as weak or unreliable.

Ironically, this makes the problem worse. ADHD does not improve under shame. Executive function does not strengthen under fear. What improves performance is structure, predictability, and environments that reduce unnecessary cognitive load. When the system refuses to acknowledge disability, it denies the very tools that would stabilize performance.

This is how capable lawyers burn out, stumble into disciplinary trouble, or leave the profession entirely. Not because they lack ability, but because the profession insists on evaluating them as if disability were irrelevant.

The Sin Framework

There is an unspoken moral narrative running underneath much of professional regulation. It treats failure as a choice. It treats inconsistency as a lack of values. It treats difficulty as evidence of insufficient commitment.

When neurological differences are interpreted through that lens, ADHD is no longer understood as a functional impairment. It is reclassified as a character flaw—something closer to a moral failure than a cognitive one.

That shift is subtle, but it is decisive. Once difficulty is moralized, support becomes indulgence, accommodation becomes excuse, and discipline feels justified long before the underlying mechanism is examined.

This is what leads some to interpret ADHD not as a neurological difference, but as a moral failure—almost as if difficulty itself were evidence of sin.

Once behavior is framed that way, the conversation narrows. The only acceptable response becomes repentance. Do better. Try harder. Fix yourself. The system does not ask whether it has contributed to the problem. It does not examine whether its expectations align with the realities of cognitive diversity.

For lawyers with ADHD, this framing is particularly dangerous. We work in a profession obsessed with precision and accountability. There is little tolerance for variance, even when that variance is predictable and well-documented.

The tragedy is not that the law demands high standards. The tragedy is that it refuses to distinguish between unwillingness and impairment.

What Disability Law Actually Requires

The ADA does not excuse lawyers from doing the work. It requires institutions to acknowledge disability and consider reasonable accommodations that allow the work to be done.

That distinction matters.

For lawyers, the essential functions of the profession include competent legal analysis, ethical judgment, client loyalty, and substantive advocacy. Administrative mechanisms surrounding those functions, such as how time is captured, how tasks are tracked, how information is organized, and how work is sequenced, are not immutable. They are systems. Systems can be adapted.

Reasonable accommodations in legal practice are rarely dramatic. They often involve external structure. Technology that prompts rather than assumes memory. Workflow design that reduces task switching. Scheduling practices that respect circadian rhythm. Clear intake limits. Defined communication channels.

None of this lowers the bar. It makes the bar reachable.

Why the Burden Falls on the Lawyer

Here is the hard truth most lawyers with ADHD learn too late. If you do not name your disability, the system will name your behavior for you.

Once a complaint is filed or a concern is raised, narratives harden quickly. Context disappears. Disability becomes an afterthought. At that stage, you are no longer explaining your brain. You are defending your character.

This is why documentation matters. Disclosure matters. Accommodation requests matter. Not because you are asking for leniency, but because you are building an accurate record. The profession will not infer disability on its own. It will infer neglect if given the opportunity.

Responsibility Reframed

None of this absolves lawyers of responsibility. It reframes it.

Responsibility, for a lawyer with ADHD, includes managing the disability proactively. That means diagnosis, treatment, systems, and boundaries. It also means recognizing when the environment or workflow is making impairment worse and addressing that before consequences accumulate.

Taking responsibility does not mean accepting shame for neurological limitations. It means refusing to let those limitations be mischaracterized as ethical failure.

That distinction is the foundation for everything that follows in this book.

Why This Chapter Comes Early

I placed this chapter here because it changes how the reader interprets every story that follows. Task paralysis, time blindness, overcommitment, people pleasing, and state-dependent performance all look different once you understand that ADHD is not a moral problem or personality quirks.

They are predictable expressions of a disability operating inside a system that was not designed for it.

If you miss that point, the rest of the book risks being read as confession. If you understand it, the book reads as diagnosis.

And diagnosis is where accountability actually begins.

Part II

Where Performance Breaks Down

Chapter 5
Task Paralysis

Initiation Failure in a Profession that
Treats Delay as Defiance

The legal system never encounters task paralysis as an internal experience. It encounters it as silence.

It shows up as the brief that was not filed when everyone assumed it would be. It shows up as the discovery response that is technically late even though the lawyer knows the material cold. It shows up as the unanswered email that grows heavier with every passing hour. It shows up as the client who calls three times in a day and gets no response, then tells someone else that their lawyer must not care.

Judges do not see paralysis. They see delay. Clerks do not see paralysis. They see noncompliance. Disciplinary counsel does not see paralysis. They see a pattern.

That is what makes task paralysis so dangerous in the practice of law. It produces outcomes that look indistinguishable from neglect, indifference, or incompetence, even when the lawyer involved is working harder than anyone else in the room.

I have watched good lawyers lose credibility not because they did not know what to do, but because they could not initiate the thing they knew needed to be done. I have watched capable attorneys create records that later became weapons against them, all because action did not occur at the moment the system expected it to occur. The system does not care what is happening inside your head. It cares about what is on the docket.

Task paralysis is not procrastination in the casual sense. It is not laziness. It is not poor work ethic. It is the failure to initiate action despite awareness of urgency, importance, and consequence. That distinction matters, but it rarely matters to the people evaluating you after the fact.

From the outside, paralysis looks like avoidance. It looks like delay without explanation. It looks like someone choosing not to act. That appearance alone can be enough to damage your standing with a court, strain a client relationship, or create a disciplinary issue that did not need to exist.

This is especially true in criminal practice, where time is rarely neutral. Deadlines are not abstract. A missed filing date can mean a client stays in jail longer. A delayed motion can mean leverage disappears. A postponed conversation can mean a case moves in a direction that cannot be undone. When action stalls, consequences move anyway.

The cruel irony is that many lawyers experiencing task paralysis are not idle. They are thinking constantly. They are reviewing the case in their heads. They are rehearsing arguments. They are refining language internally. They are planning how they will do the work once they start. From the outside, none of that counts. The only thing that counts is movement.

This is where task paralysis quietly intersects with professional risk. Not because paralysis is misconduct, but because the system interprets its effects as misconduct. It does not distinguish between inability to initiate and refusal to act. It does not ask whether the lawyer was frozen rather than careless. It records outcomes, not causes.

By the time someone asks what happened, the damage is often already done. The deadline is missed. The client is angry. The judge is frustrated. The file contains gaps that now require explanation. Task paralysis is rarely forgiven because it is rarely understood.

That is why this chapter begins here, with consequence rather than feeling. Before we talk about what paralysis feels like from the inside, it is essential to understand what it produces on the outside. Only then does the internal experience make sense in the context of professional reality.

Because task paralysis does not announce itself as a struggle. It announces itself as a failure.

When I talk about task paralysis, I am not talking about ordinary procrastination. I am talking about a specific and familiar state where the work is in front of you, you understand its importance, and your brain simply will not move. Not forward. Not sideways. Not at all.

This is the loop. You see the task. You know it matters. You do not start. Shame follows almost immediately. That shame raises the emotional stakes of the task, which makes starting even harder. The cycle repeats until the work feels poisonous and you begin questioning your own competence rather than the condition you are actually dealing with.

I have been caught in that loop more times than I care to admit. It has happened on briefs, trial preparation, bond motions, and even on routine communications that should have taken minutes instead of hours. So when I talk about how to break paralysis, I am not offering theory or productivity folklore. I am describing what I do on the days when my own brain feels immovable. This is not a cure. It is a field guide.

The first thing I have learned is to name the condition instead of attacking myself. The instinct, especially in lawyers, is self prosecution. Why am I like this. Real lawyers do not struggle with this. If I do not get moving right now, I am going to blow everything up. That internal cross examination never helps. It raises the stakes until the task feels dangerous rather than manageable.

What helps is separating identity from condition. There is a meaningful difference between saying I am failing and saying I am in paralysis. When I catch myself opening the same document repeatedly without producing anything, I try to name it plainly. I am stuck. This is ADHD interfering with initiation. That shift matters. Naming the problem pulls it out of the shame spiral and into the category of something that can be addressed. Precision calms the nervous system. Vague self condemnation does the opposite.

The second move is shrinking the task until my brain stops lying to me. The ADHD brain is very good at inflating a single assignment into something overwhelming. Writing a brief becomes researching case law, perfecting structure, anticipating judicial reaction, worrying about consequences, and replaying prior mistakes. No wonder the brain freezes. It is responding to perceived threat, not workload.

When I am truly stuck, I stop asking whether I can complete the task and start asking what the smallest responsible step is that does not trigger resistance. Not writing the motion. Opening the document and inserting the caption. Not preparing for trial. Pulling the indictment and listing the charges on paper. The step has to be small enough that my brain cannot convincingly argue that it is impossible. If I find myself debating whether the step is too much, it still is.

Another critical lesson is removing decisions before paralysis sets in. Most paralysis is not caused by difficulty. It is caused by choice overload. Where do I start. Which format do I use. What tone is right. What if this is wrong. That entire debate happens before the first word is typed.

This is why templates matter. This is why trial notebooks matter. This is why standard formats are not laziness but survival tools. When I can open a document that already has structure, headings, and placeholders, my brain has fewer exits. Every decision made in advance is one less opportunity to freeze.

Time also has to be made smaller than the task. I have learned that negotiating with hours is a losing game on bad days. Instead, I work in defined blocks. Twenty four minutes. I am not trying to finish anything in that window. I am committing to staying with the same file and the same task until the timer ends. If I drift, I notice it, reset, and return.

Some sessions produce good work. Some produce very little. But even on the worst days, that container prevents shame from spreading. I did not fail the entire day. I had a difficult twenty four minutes. That distinction keeps me in the fight.

Environment matters more than most lawyers are willing to admit. Lighting, sound, visual clutter, they are not background conditions. They directly affect cognitive load. There have been afternoons when nothing moved at my desk, but walking outside with one file and a legal pad unlocked the work almost immediately.

When I notice that I have been stuck through multiple attempts, I change the setting before I change the task. I stand up. I clear my immediate visual field. I adjust the light. I take one physical item related to the work and relocate. This is not indulgence. It is adaptation.

Another effective interruption is involving one other human being early. Paralysis thrives in secrecy. The temptation is to stay silent and hope for a last minute breakthrough. Sometimes that works. Sometimes it turns a manageable delay into a real problem.

A simple disclosure helps. I am having trouble getting started on this brief. I am going to work on it for the next half hour and will follow up once I have the first section drafted. That creates a witness. Lawyers understand the power of a witness. Accountability does not cure ADHD, but it disrupts the fantasy that paralysis can continue indefinitely without consequence.

Finally, there are days when powering through is not the answer. There are moments when the brain is genuinely depleted, not avoidant. On those days, the responsible move is to do the smallest defensible step and plan a real attempt later. That might mean outlining instead of drafting. It might mean sending a message that resets expectations within ethical bounds. It does not mean ignoring obligations or blaming ADHD for missed deadlines.

Part of living with this brain is learning to distinguish avoidance from exhaustion. That line is not always clear. I get it wrong. But the more I practice noticing and adjusting, the less time I spend frozen in place.

If there is one thing to take from this section, it is this. Task paralysis is not evidence that you are unfit to practice law. It is evidence that you are practicing in an environment that places extraordinary cognitive demands on a brain wired differently. This book exists because too many lawyers are fighting that battle alone.

You will not win every day. I do not. But you can build a set of responses for the moments when motion feels impossible. Sometimes that is enough to shift the balance away from shame and back toward movement.

Why Lawyers Are Especially Vulnerable to Task Paralysis

Task paralysis hits lawyers differently than it hits most other professionals, and pretending otherwise is part of the problem. The law is not a field that tolerates partial effort, visible uncertainty, or exploratory drafts. You do not get credit for being close. You get judged on what is filed, what is said, and what is preserved on the record.

That reality matters for a brain that struggles with initiation.

In many professions, starting messy is acceptable. You can sketch ideas, throw something on a whiteboard, test a version, and refine later. Legal work rarely works that way. A motion filed too early can lock you into a position you cannot escape. A poorly worded email can become an exhibit. A half-formed argument can cost credibility with a judge who will remember it long after you have moved on.

For an ADHD brain, that level of consequence raises the cost of beginning. Starting does not feel neutral. It feels dangerous.

Layer on top of that the ambiguity built into legal work. Rarely is there a single correct answer. Strategy choices involve judgment calls, tradeoffs, and unknown reactions from judges and opposing counsel. The ADHD brain does not freeze because it lacks ideas. It freezes because it sees too many paths at once, all of them carrying potential risk.

Then there is time pressure. Deadlines in law are not suggestions. They carry sanctions, professional embarrassment, and in extreme cases, discipline. Knowing that something matters does not always help. Often it makes the paralysis worse. The task becomes heavier, louder, and more difficult to approach without triggering panic.

From the outside, this looks like delay. From the inside, it feels like standing in front of a door that you know you must open, while your nervous system is screaming that what is on the other side could harm you.

This is why telling a lawyer with ADHD to "just start" is rarely helpful. The resistance is not to work. It is to exposure. Exposure to being wrong. Exposure to being judged. Exposure to consequences that cannot be undone.

Understanding that distinction matters, because without it, task paralysis gets mislabeled. Judges see it as neglect. Colleagues see it as unreliability. Clients see it as indifference. The lawyer experiencing it sees it as personal failure.

In reality, it is a predictable response to practicing law in an environment that punishes uncertainty while demanding constant output. That does not excuse missed deadlines or poor communication. But it does explain why otherwise capable lawyers find themselves frozen in ways that do not match their intelligence or commitment.

When Paralysis Turns Into Patterns

Task paralysis rarely stays contained. Left unmanaged, it does not simply repeat itself. It evolves.

When a lawyer experiences paralysis often enough, they start compensating for it. They stay late. They work in bursts of intensity. They rely on adrenaline instead of planning. They tell themselves they function best under pressure, even as the pressure grows heavier and more constant.

This is how paralysis quietly feeds other patterns that look unrelated on the surface.

Overcommitment often comes next. Saying yes feels easier than facing the discomfort of starting what is already on the desk. Taking on one more obligation creates the illusion of movement, even as existing tasks remain untouched. The calendar fills. The workload expands. The underlying paralysis remains.

People pleasing follows closely behind. When work gets delayed, anxiety rises. The instinct becomes smoothing things over. Promising quick turnarounds. Offering reassurance instead of timelines. Avoiding hard conversations in favor of temporary relief.

From the outside, this looks like poor time management. From the inside, it is a survival strategy.

None of this happens because the lawyer stopped caring. It happens because the nervous system learned that urgency temporarily overrides paralysis. Crisis becomes the only reliable ignition source. That is not a sustainable way to practice law, but it is a common one.

This is why task paralysis cannot be treated as an isolated productivity issue. It is an early warning sign. If ignored, it reshapes how a lawyer works, how they relate to clients, and how they interact with the system that judges their performance.

The goal is not to eliminate paralysis entirely. That is unrealistic. The goal is to recognize it early, respond to it deliberately, and prevent it from cascading into patterns that create real professional risk.

Because once paralysis stops being episodic and starts driving behavior, the consequences stop being internal. They show up on dockets, in emails, and eventually, in places no lawyer ever wants their name to appear.

That is the point where task paralysis stops being an internal struggle and starts reshaping how a lawyer practices. What comes next is not a separate set of problems. It is the fallout.

Chapter 6
Time Blindness
How ADHD Distorts Urgency, Duration, and Consequence

Time is supposed to be the one thing in a lawyer's life that does not bend. Deadlines are fixed. Court starts when it starts. Discovery closes when the rule says it closes. Judges expect you to appear in their courtroom at the precise minute listed on the docket, regardless of what else is happening in your day or in your head. The profession runs on the assumption that every lawyer experiences time the same way, that we all carry the same internal clock, that urgency rises and falls in predictable increments.

My brain never agreed to those terms.

I do not experience time as a straight line. I experience it as pressure and relief, as threat and calm. Time shows up in my nervous system, not on a watch. That difference has shaped my entire professional life, often in ways I did not understand until much later. Long before I had language for it, I knew I was slightly out of sync with the people around me, like I was hearing the same music at a different tempo.

That mismatch has consequences in a profession that treats time as absolute.

There are days when hours disappear without leaving a trace. Not because I am distracted or unproductive. Sometimes I am working harder than I ever have. I am reading, thinking, outlining, chasing threads that feel important and necessary. Then I look up and half the day is gone. The shock is real every time. I am stunned, because internally it feels like twenty minutes passed, not four hours.

Other days, time crawls. Fifteen minutes stretches into something that feels like an entire afternoon. A deadline weeks away sits quietly on the calendar, weightless, until one morning it lands on my chest with full force. The urgency arrives all at once, without warning. It is not gradual. It is not polite. It is immediate and overwhelming.

That is time blindness.

There was a day early in my practice when I walked into the office convinced I was ahead.

Nothing dramatic was scheduled. No trial. No hearings. Just a short list of things I had been meaning to knock out before the end of the week. A response to an email. A draft motion that wasn't due yet. A file I wanted to review before a client meeting the following week. The kind of day lawyers tell themselves they'll "finally catch up."

I remember sitting down at my desk with coffee still warm, opening a file, and thinking, Good. This won't take long.

I was working. Reading carefully. Taking notes. Following threads that felt relevant. Every so often I would look up, satisfied that I was making progress, that familiar sense that things were under control. At some point, the building got quieter.

I didn't notice right away. I was focused. Engaged. In the middle of something that felt important, even if I couldn't have told you exactly what I would have produced by the end of it.

When I finally looked at the clock, it felt like a mistake. I checked my phone to confirm. Then the computer. Then the wall clock, as if the time might change depending on where I looked.

It was late afternoon.

Not late in the sense of the day is moving along, but late in the sense that something had already been lost. The kind of late where you start mentally rearranging what now has to wait, what will spill into tomorrow, what will quietly slide another day down the calendar.

I felt the familiar mix of confusion and self-reproach.

What did I do all day?

The unsettling part wasn't that I hadn't worked. I had. I was mentally tired. My notes were detailed. The file was marked up. But nothing concrete had crossed the finish line. No email sent. No draft saved. No visible marker that time had passed in the way the rest of the world understands it.

From the outside, it would have looked like a normal workday. From the inside, it felt like time had folded in on itself.

That was one of the first moments I can remember realizing that my problem was not effort, or intelligence, or commitment.

It was that time did not register while I was inside it. The future never tapped me on the shoulder. The present never warned me it was moving. The day didn't fall apart.

But it slipped.

And I would spend years after that blaming myself for something I could not yet name.

It is not procrastination. It is not indifference. It is not a failure of caring. It is a neurological disconnect between the passage of time and the emotional signals that normally tell a person when to begin, when to continue, and when to stop. Knowledge alone does not move the clock. Emotion does.

I have lived with this as long as I can remember. I lived with it in college, where papers appeared due out of nowhere. I lived with it in law school, where I could prepare for an exam in a single, brutal stretch and still feel blindsided by the calendar. I lived with it during trials, where the stakes were too high to admit that my internal sense of time did not match the court's expectations. I lived with it while juggling hearings, clients, investigators, and dockets that kept expanding even when my perception of time did not.

I lived with it when the disciplinary system came knocking and assumed, incorrectly, that my relationship to time was a matter of character.

Time blindness is not about character. It is about neurology. It is about how an ADHD brain perceives duration and consequence. Most people have an intuitive sense of how long they have been engaged in a task. They can feel time moving. They can sense when a deadline is approaching even if they are not staring at a calendar. That internal signal nudges them forward before panic is required.

I do not have that signal. My brain does not reliably register the passage of time unless emotion pulls it into focus. Calm tasks stay invisible. Future obligations remain abstract. The present moment crowds everything else out. The result is a professional life full of unintended surprises.

You think you have days left to prepare a hearing and suddenly it is tomorrow morning. You believe you will return calls before lunch and the building is closing. You sit down intending to draft a routine motion and discover that the sun is rising and you have been working through the night without realizing it.

Each realization feels like stepping into cold water. The shock never dulls.

Once, a colleague asked how I managed to prepare for trial on short notice. I told him the truth, although I did not understand it fully at the time. I said I did not do it on purpose. I simply did not feel the urgency until the world narrowed enough to force it. When that moment arrives, my brain can lock in with frightening intensity. I can read hundreds of pages of discovery in a single night. I can build a theory of defense with a clarity that surprises even me.

From the outside, that looks like mastery.

What people do not see is the cost. They do not see the panic that comes from realizing too late that the preparation window has almost closed. They do not see the exhaustion that follows when adrenaline finally drains away. They do not see the shame that settles in afterward, the quiet belief that if you were more disciplined, more organized, more like everyone else, you would not live this way.

Time blindness is not a quirk. It is the engine behind missed deadlines, behind unanswered emails, behind the nights when work only ignites because the pressure finally became unbearable. It is the engine that drives inconsistency, and inconsistency is the one sin the legal profession has very little patience for.

There is something uniquely unforgiving about how time blindness collides with law. In many jobs, there is flexibility in when work is completed. In law, the calendar controls everything. The law does not care how your brain experiences time. It cares whether the filing is late. It cares whether the client feels ignored. It cares whether you were standing in the courtroom when your case was called.

The profession measures time mechanically. Performance is measured by outcomes. Filings are either timely or late. Communication is either prompt or deficient. Explanations matter less than results.

When something slips, the profession reaches for familiar interpretations. Carelessness. Poor prioritization. Failure to manage workload. Those labels are not usually malicious. They are simply incomplete. They describe what happened without asking why.

There were mornings in my career when I fully intended to respond to discovery before lunch. I would sit down at my desk, open the file, and begin reading. A fact would catch my attention. A question would need answering. I would follow that trail, doing what any careful advocate would do. Hours later, I would surface and realize the day had vanished.

I was not avoiding the work. I was working. I simply did not feel the clock moving.

Time blindness also reshapes life outside the courtroom. There were nights when I sat down intending to spend two hours preparing for trial and found myself at sunrise surrounded by open files. I was not drifting. I was not disengaged. I was fully immersed. Time became elastic. It stretched and collapsed without warning. Breaks never arrived because I never felt them coming.

Anyone who lives with time blindness learns quickly that calendars alone do not fix it. Reminders alone do not fix it. The problem is not ignorance of deadlines. The problem is delayed temporal awareness. The future does not carry emotional weight. The present does not carry duration. Only crisis feels real.

This is why people with ADHD are often drawn to high-pressure environments. Trial work offers something the rest of the world does not. It offers immediacy. Stakes are visible. Consequences are sitting ten feet away. Emotion writes the schedule. When the judge says court resumes at 1:30, my brain feels that. When a witness finishes answering and cross-examination begins, time snaps into focus.

In those moments, my perception of time aligns with what the profession expects.

Outside the courtroom, the cues are softer. They require an internal signal my brain does not reliably generate. That is why task paralysis and time blindness blend together so easily. If the brain cannot sense time, it cannot sense when to begin. Overwhelm dulls initiation. Delayed initiation compresses urgency. The cycle feeds itself.

The disciplinary world does not understand this cycle. It sees the late filing without knowing how many times you started it. It sees the communication gap without understanding that every intention to reply was real. It sees inconsistency where there was effort. It sees indifference where there was fear.

Time blindness is recognized under federal law as a functional impairment because it affects major life activities, including working. It affects planning, organizing, prioritizing, remembering, and executing. Those are not peripheral skills in law. They are woven into daily practice.

That recognition matters, not as an excuse, but as a framework. Disability does not erase responsibility. It shapes what responsibility looks like in practice. It explains why effort does not always translate cleanly into outcome. It demands a different analysis than moral judgment alone.

The truth is that many lawyers with ADHD are exceptional under pressure. They shine when the heat is on. They think quickly, read people well, and adapt in real time. The courtroom rewards exactly that kind of mind. The office punishes it. One environment provides structure and immediacy. The other demands self-generated time awareness.

The problem is not that one version of the lawyer is real and the other is fake. Both are real. Both exist at the same time.

The point of talking about time blindness in a book like this is not to justify the past. It is to name something many lawyers live with in silence. It is to give shape to a problem the profession often refuses to acknowledge. It is to say that the expectations placed on lawyers are built around a brain that processes time in a way many of us do not share.

There will always be people who hear the phrase time blindness and assume it means someone is not trying. They are wrong. Time blindness means effort does not reliably produce the expected timing. It means the internal clock most people rely on is unreliable or absent. Without external structure, time becomes unmoored.

Living this way is exhausting. It reshapes your relationship with work, with colleagues, with clients, and with yourself. It creates a constant low-grade anxiety that no amount of talent can fully quiet. It forces you to question whether your best effort will ever be enough in a profession built on punctuality.

Yet time blindness is not the whole story. It is one part of a system that can be rebuilt. It exists alongside strengths that the profession often celebrates when it sees them up close. The goal is not to fix the brain. The goal is to understand it well enough to stop fighting it blindly.

You cannot manage what you do not recognize. You cannot design around something you insist is a moral flaw. Time blindness means time is subjective, emotional, and unpredictable. It can be managed, but not through willpower alone. It requires structure, intention, and acknowledgment.

Once you understand how distorted time perception operates, the usual advice starts to sound thin. Use a calendar. Plan better. Be more disciplined. Those tools help at the margins, but they do not address the deeper problem. The problem is not that time slips. The problem is that time does not register with appropriate weight until it is too late.

This chapter exists to make that reality visible. Before you can change how you work, you have to understand how time works inside your own head. What makes time blindness truly dangerous is not the lost hours themselves, but what happens when all that lost time suddenly demands payment at once.

That is where the real damage begins.

Chapter 7
Time Blindness II
When Thirty Days Collapse
Into Thirty Minutes

Time blindness rarely announces itself as failure. For most of a lawyer's career, it operates quietly in the background, producing friction rather than catastrophe. Work gets done. Deadlines are usually met. Clients are mostly satisfied. From the outside, there is little reason to suspect that anything fundamental is wrong.

That is what makes it dangerous. Time blindness does not show up as an inability to work. It shows up as an inability to feel the future. Deadlines exist intellectually but lack emotional weight until they are close enough to cause pain. The calendar moves forward whether the nervous system registers it or not, and eventually the two collide.

When they do, the experience is jarring. A deadline that has existed for weeks suddenly feels immediate. Not because new information has appeared, but because the brain has finally received the signal it needs to act. The problem is that the signal arrives too late to leave margin.

This is the version of time blindness that creates real professional risk. Not the mild disorganization that can be patched with an apology or a late night, but the collapse of temporal awareness that turns a manageable obligation into an emergency.

I've Got Time, and other Fictions ADHD Brains tell Itself.

There's a particular kind of reassurance that I've told myself more times than I can count.

Not the intentional kind. Not the kind you tell other people. The kind you tell yourself because it feels soothing, because it keeps you upright, because the alternative is admitting you're about to drive the whole week straight into a wall.

I've got time. It almost feels like a soothing bedtime story you tell yourself when nothing feels urgent yet.

It happened on a day that should have been easy. No trial. No jury. No emergency walk-in client asking the kind of question that makes your throat tighten. Just paper. Deadlines. The quiet administrative stuff that keeps a practice from turning into a junk drawer.

The deadline was out there — thirty days away on the calendar — clean and distant. It wasn't screaming. It wasn't glowing red. It was just a number sitting politely in the future. I could see it. I knew it mattered. I was even proud of myself for noticing it early.

I remember thinking, This time I'm going to do it right. I'm going to start early like a normal person.

And I meant it.

I opened the case file. I made a couple notes. I flagged a couple issues. I even created a document with the caption so I wouldn't have to do it later. That tiny act was supposed to be my "start." It was supposed to be proof I was ahead.

Then the day did what days do.

A client call turned into a longer call. A "quick question" from another case became a problem that needed a real answer. I got pulled into court on something that wasn't technically mine, but it needed a lawyer with a pulse and a tie. Then a prosecutor sent an email that looked harmless until you read it twice and realized it was bait. Then an investigator needed direction. Then a judge moved something on the docket and suddenly I had a hearing I didn't expect.

Nothing was catastrophic.

That's the point. The month didn't collapse because of one dramatic event. It collapsed through ordinary life, the slow drip of small demands that carry just enough urgency to hijack attention.

Every day, that deadline sat quietly in the distance like a billboard on a highway you weren't on yet. You could see it, but it didn't touch you. It didn't press on your body. It didn't create the feeling that makes action happen.

If someone asked me during that time whether I was "on top of it," I would have said yes without blinking. Because in my head, I was.

The belief that I had time wasn't reckless or irrational. It was based on the information that my brain had at that moment. It was the quiet calendar, no immediate pressure, and the absence of any internal alarm.

I was tracking it. I was aware. I had a plan. I just hadn't started in the way people mean when they say "start." I had done the ADHD version of starting—thinking about it, circling it, touching the edges of it, imagining the finished product, rehearsing the steps. I had carried it around like a weight in my pocket and mistaken that weight for progress.

And then, one morning, something shifted.

Not the work. Not the law. Not the facts. My nervous system.

I sat at my desk and looked at the calendar, and the deadline—which had been a quiet, distant concept—suddenly had teeth. It moved from "future" to "now" in the span of a single glance. My chest tightened. My mind did that thing where it starts counting the hours left, and then counting the other obligations stacked on top of those hours, and then doing the math you don't want to do because you already know where it ends.

Thirty days didn't feel like thirty days. It felt like thirty minutes.

That's what people misunderstand. They think time blindness means you forget. They think you don't care. They think you're coasting until the last second because you like drama.

But it wasn't drama. It was a delayed signal.

The deadline hadn't changed. *I* hadn't changed. The calendar had been marching toward it every day. I had been living inside those days. I had been working hard. I had been busy.

What I had not been was activated.

Now I was. And when the panic hit, it didn't arrive alone. Panic never arrives alone.

Because once one deadline becomes real, your brain finally checks the rest of the calendar too. And suddenly you see the other things you agreed to while the future still felt open. The hearing you thought was next week. The client meeting that's closer than you remembered. The email you meant to send "today." The call you promised you'd return. The draft you told yourself you would knock out in "an hour."

They all show up at the same time, like a rambling herd.

I remember staring at my desk—not blank, not disorganized, but crowded. Files stacked, notes everywhere, a computer screen full of open documents that all represented something unfinished. Not because I hadn't worked. Because I had worked on too many things without crossing a finish line.

That's when I did what I always do when urgency finally hits.

I went into emergency mode. The day became a tunnel. The world narrowed. The phone felt like an enemy. Every new email was an insult. I stopped eating without meaning to. I stopped drinking water without noticing. The only thing that existed was the deadline and the shame riding shotgun.

And here's the part no one sees: the urgency that finally makes you productive also strips you of margin. You're not just working. You're working in a way that leaves no room for error.

There's no space to step back and ask, *Is this the best argument?* There's no time to rewrite for clarity. There's no buffer for the curveball—an unexpected filing, a client crisis, a missing document. You're drafting like someone trying to outrun a closing door.

You can be brilliant in that state. You can produce good work. You can look, from the outside, like the lawyer who "really shines under pressure."

That pressure always comes due.

Because even if you win, even if you file on time, even if the judge never knows how close you were to disaster, you pay for it afterward. The adrenaline drains. The exhaustion hits. The shame stays. And you have to pretend you weren't just in a private war with the calendar.

The worst part is what happens next. You file. You survive. You get past it. And the system rewards that survival as proof the system was right.

See? He got it done.

No one sees the cost. No one sees the frantic hours. No one sees the way your brain had to be threatened into functioning. No one sees how unsustainable it is to run a practice on last-minute ignition.

And you don't explain it. You can't.

Because the explanation sounds like weakness in a profession that worships control. It sounds like excuse in a system that measures outcomes, not mechanisms. It sounds like you're asking for special treatment when all you really want is for someone to understand that your internal clock does not send warning signals in a normal sequence.

So you do what you've always done. You reset the lie, that belief.

Next time I'll start earlier.

And for a while, you believe it. Not because you're naive. Because you want to be free.   But then thirty days comes again. Quiet. Distant. Weightless. And if you don't build structure that makes the future real before panic is required, the month disappears the same way it always does. Not in a blaze.

In a blur.

The Long Calm Before the Panic

One of the most confusing aspects of time blindness is how calm it feels right up until the moment it doesn't. There is no gradual increase in urgency. No steady tightening of focus. For long stretches, the deadline feels distant, almost hypothetical. You know it exists, but it does not press on you. It does not intrude on your thinking. It does not demand action.

That calm is deceptive. In a neurotypical brain, urgency builds in stages. A deadline a month away feels different than one a week away. The pressure increases as the window narrows, prompting earlier preparation. For an ADHD brain, that middle ground is largely absent. The deadline stays emotionally flat until it is suddenly on top of you.

This is not forgetfulness. It is not denial. It is a failure of temporal signaling. The future does not send a reliable message to the present.

As a result, work tends to cluster. You may spend days or weeks handling what feels most immediate while believing there is still time to address everything else. That belief is not reckless. It is sincere. The brain genuinely experiences the future as open, right up to the moment it closes.

Why "Just Start Earlier" Fails

Advice about time management almost always assumes that awareness leads to action. Start earlier. Plan ahead. Break the task into steps. All of that presumes that the future already feels real enough to motivate behavior.

For someone with time blindness, that assumption does not hold.

You can understand, perfectly well, that starting earlier would be better. You can intend to do so. You can even plan to do so. What is missing is the internal cue that says now is the moment to begin. Without that cue, initiation stalls.

This is why time blindness is so often misread as procrastination. From the outside, it looks like delay. From the inside, it feels like waiting for a signal that never arrives. When the signal finally does arrive, it arrives with force.

The Panic Activation Window

When a deadline crosses the threshold from abstract to immediate, the ADHD brain often snaps into focus with startling intensity. Dopamine surges. Distractions fall away. The mind narrows onto the task with a clarity that can look, from the outside, like discipline finally kicking in. This is the paradox that keeps the cycle alive.

Under pressure, many lawyers with ADHD do excellent work. They write quickly. They think sharply. They perform at a high level. The output can be impressive enough to reinforce the belief that this is simply how they work best.

What gets overlooked is the cost. Work done in panic leaves no margin. There is no room for revision. No space for error. No buffer for interruption. The quality may be high, but the risk is higher. One unexpected obstacle, one miscalculation, one competing emergency, and the entire structure collapses.

The profession tends to reward the visible performance while ignoring the invisible strain that produced it.

The Illusion of Staying Ahead

For a long time, it can feel like you are managing the problem. You learn which fires must be handled immediately and which can wait. You rely on experience and intuition to keep things moving. You stay just ahead of disaster, convincing yourself that you have found a workable rhythm.

That rhythm is fragile. The system depends on pressure to function, and pressure does not scale. When obligations increase, urgency stops organizing attention and starts fragmenting it. Instead of clarifying priorities, it creates competition between them.

At that point, work shifts from planning to triage. Decisions are no longer about what deserves care, but about what will cause the least damage if it waits. Nothing about this feels negligent in the moment. It feels necessary.

The problem is that triage is not a sustainable operating mode for a profession built on precision.

Why Consequences Arrive All at Once

Time blindness compresses outcomes. Instead of small corrections spread across time, consequences tend to cluster. Deadlines that felt unrelated collide. Court dates stack. Client demands overlap. The calendar becomes crowded all at once, even though the commitments were made gradually. This is often experienced as shock.

You look at the week ahead and wonder how it filled so quickly. You feel blindsided by obligations you do not remember agreeing to, even though you did. The future never felt crowded while those commitments were accumulating. It only feels crowded when there is no room left.

That is when others begin to notice. From the outside, it looks like a pattern of neglect emerging suddenly. From the inside, it feels like being ambushed by time itself.

How the Profession Interprets the Collision

The legal system is not designed to ask how time is perceived. It measures conduct mechanically. Filings are timely or late. Communication is prompt or deficient. Explanations matter less than outcomes.

When things begin to slip, familiar narratives appear. Disorganization. Poor prioritization. Failure to manage a practice. These interpretations are not usually malicious. They are simply incomplete.

What they miss is the role distorted time perception played upstream.

The lawyer did not ignore the deadline. The deadline never generated urgency until it was too close. The lawyer did not choose chaos. The future never felt full when the commitments were made. By the time the consequences appear, those distinctions no longer matter. The system responds to what it can see.

That is why time blindness becomes dangerous long before it becomes obvious.

Emergency Mode as a Trap

Many lawyers with ADHD learn to rely on emergency mode because it works. Under pressure, focus improves. Performance sharpens. Distraction recedes. Crisis creates clarity.

Over time, emergency mode starts to feel like competence. What it actually does is exhaust the system that makes competence possible.

Living in constant urgency erodes judgment. Recovery time disappears. Every task becomes a fire drill. Eventually, the nervous system loses the ability to reset. Focus becomes harder to access without stress, and stress becomes harder to escape once engaged.

This is often when shame enters the picture. You know you are capable of better. You remember periods when the work flowed and the mind cooperated. You look at the pileup and blame yourself for not staying ahead of it. You work longer hours. You sleep less. You promise that next time will be different.

Shame does not fix the problem. It deepens it.

Why the Pattern Repeats

Time blindness does not resolve through insight alone. Knowing what went wrong does not change how the future feels. Good intentions do not make distant deadlines emotionally real. Promising to start earlier does not generate the internal signal required to begin.

The cycle resets because the underlying mechanism remains unchanged.

Deferred initiation leads to compressed urgency. Compressed urgency leads to overload. Overload produces visible failure. The response is renewed determination rather than structural change, and the pattern runs again. Until something interrupts it.

Why This Chapter Comes Before Overcommitment

Time blindness is what allows overcommitment to feel harmless. When the future feels open, saying yes feels safe.

When deadlines lack emotional weight, adding one more obligation does not register as costly.

Overcommitment is rarely a conscious decision to do too much. It is the byproduct of distorted forecasting. The cost of the commitment does not feel real when the commitment is made.

By the time the collision occurs, the commitments are already locked in.

Understanding this matters because it shifts the analysis away from blame and toward design. If the problem were simply effort, effort would have fixed it by now. The issue lies upstream, in how time is experienced and how future obligations are evaluated.

The Warning Inside the Pattern

Time blindness does not announce itself as disability. It presents as optimism. It presents as confidence in future focus. It presents as a belief that things will come together later.

That is what makes it dangerous in a profession that values reliability above all else.

The collision follows a pattern that can be anticipated once it is recognized. Ignoring that pattern does not make you resilient. It leaves you exposed.

Lawyers with ADHD do not need to become different people to solve this problem. They need structures that make time visible, commitments costly to accept, and future obligations harder to ignore.

That work begins by confronting how easily capacity is overestimated when time does not feel real.

Where This Leaves Us

If this chapter feels uncomfortably familiar, that reaction makes sense. It describes a failure mode many lawyers recognize but rarely name.

The next chapter turns toward what happens when distorted time perception collides with professional identity. Overcommitment does not grow out of recklessness or ego. It grows out of optimism combined with time blindness.

Until that connection is addressed, the cycle will continue. This chapter ends where the next one must begin, at the moment where saying yes still feels safe and the future still feels empty.

Chapter 8
Time Blindness III
Borrowed Time: When Everything Comes Due at Once

For a long time, time blindness does not feel dangerous.

It feels inconvenient. It feels irritating. It creates moments of embarrassment that can usually be smoothed over with a late night, an apology, or a burst of last-minute productivity. Deadlines are missed by inches, not miles. Messages are returned eventually. From the outside, everything still looks functional.

You show up. You argue well. You produce results.

The wheels do not come off all at once. They loosen gradually, one small wobble at a time, until the day they finally hit the pavement.

That day rarely arrives as a single failure. It arrives as convergence.

A hearing lands closer than you expected. A filing deadline you planned to start early now overlaps two others. A client wants an answer now, not later. A judge wants a response before you have time to gather your thoughts. Each of these obligations would be manageable on its own. Together, they overwhelm the fragile system you have been using to keep time at bay.

This is the point where time blindness stops being private strain and becomes visible risk.

The Illusion of Staying Ahead

Most lawyers with ADHD survive for years by living just ahead of disaster.

They keep enough plates spinning to maintain appearances. They develop instincts for what must be handled immediately and what can be deferred another day. They rely on pressure to pull focus into alignment. That approach works until the volume of obligation exceeds what urgency can organize.

Pressure does not scale.

When too many obligations demand attention at once, urgency stops functioning as a compass and starts acting like static. The mind shifts from planning to triage. You are no longer deciding what deserves care. You are deciding what will cause the least damage if it waits.

Administrative work suffers first. Documentation slips. Communication becomes reactive instead of intentional. Nothing about this feels reckless in the moment. It feels necessary. You tell yourself you will circle back once the fire is out.

The problem is that the fires keep multiplying.

What once felt like staying ahead now feels like running in place. The margin you relied on disappears quietly. Tasks begin colliding rather than lining up. The calendar fills faster than your nervous system can process. And still, from the outside, you look busy, engaged, committed.

That illusion is one of the most dangerous features of time blindness.

Why Consequences Arrive in Clusters

Time blindness compresses consequences.

Instead of small corrections spread across weeks, accountability arrives all at once. Deadlines that once felt unrelated collide. Court dates stack. Client expectations overlap. Client expectations overlap. Court dates stack. Filing deadlines that once felt unrelated suddenly occupy the same narrow window. The calendar becomes crowded all at once, even though the commitments were made gradually, over weeks or months.

When this happens, the experience is often one of genuine shock.

Not because the obligations are unreasonable. Not because the lawyer forgot they existed. But because the future never felt full while those commitments were accumulating. It only feels full when there is no room left.

That is the moment when others begin to notice.

From the outside, it looks like a pattern of neglect emerging out of nowhere. From the inside, it feels like being ambushed by obligations you do not remember agreeing to, even though you did. The difference is not awareness. It is timing. The cost of those commitments did not register until they all came due at once.

By the time the collision occurs, explanation no longer matters. The system responds to what it can see.

How the Profession Reads the Moment

The legal profession is not built to ask how time is experienced. It measures conduct by outcomes. Filings are either timely or late. Communication is either prompt or deficient. Calendars either were respected or they were not.

When things begin to slip, the profession reaches for familiar interpretations. Disorganization. Poor prioritization. Failure to manage a practice. None of those labels are malicious. They are simply incomplete.

What they miss is the role time perception played in getting there.

The lawyer did not ignore the deadline. The deadline never generated urgency until it was too close. The lawyer did not choose chaos. The future never felt crowded when the commitments were made. By the time the consequences appear, those distinctions no longer matter. The system responds to results, not process.

This is why time blindness becomes dangerous long before it becomes obvious.

Emergency Mode and Its Cost

Many lawyers with ADHD learn to rely on emergency mode.

They know they can perform under pressure. They have proven it repeatedly. Trials, hearings, crises—these sharpen focus and quiet distraction. Emergency mode feels competent. It feels decisive. It feels like proof that everything is under control.

What it actually does is exhaust the system that makes performance possible.

Living in constant urgency drains judgment. It erodes recovery time. It turns every task into a fire drill. Over time, the nervous system loses the ability to reset. Focus becomes harder to access without stress, and stress becomes harder to escape once engaged.

This is often when shame enters the picture.

The lawyer knows they are capable of better. They remember days when the work flowed and the mind cooperated. They look at the pileup and blame themselves for not staying ahead of it. They work longer hours. They sleep less. They promise themselves that next time will be different.

The cycle tightens rather than resolves.

Why the Pattern Repeats

Time blindness does not correct itself through insight.

Knowing what went wrong does not change how the future feels. Good intentions do not make distant deadlines emotionally real. Promising to start earlier does not generate the internal signal needed to begin.

Deferred initiation leads to compressed urgency. Compressed urgency leads to overload. Overload leads to visible failure. The cycle resets with renewed determination, only to run again.

This repetition is not stubbornness. It is predictability.

Why This Chapter Comes Before Overcommitment

Time blindness is the condition that allows overcommitment to take root.

When the future feels open, saying yes feels harmless. When deadlines do not register with emotional weight, adding one more obligation does not feel risky. Capacity is evaluated without access to future cost.

Overcommitment is rarely a conscious decision to do too much. It is a byproduct of distorted forecasting. The consequences do not feel real when the commitment is made.

By the time the collision occurs, the commitments are already locked in.

Understanding this matters because it shifts the focus away from blame and toward design. If the problem were simply effort, effort would have fixed it by now. The issue lives upstream, in how time is perceived and how obligations are evaluated.

The Warning Inside the Pattern

Time blindness does not announce itself as disability.

It presents as competence right up until the moment it doesn't. That is what makes it so dangerous in a profession that values reliability above all else. The collapse is not random. It follows a pattern that can be anticipated once it is recognized.

Ignoring that pattern does not make you resilient. It leaves you exposed.

Lawyers with ADHD do not need to become different people to solve this problem. They need structures that make time visible, commitments costly to accept, and future obligations harder to ignore.

That work begins by confronting how easily capacity is overestimated when time does not feel real.

What Comes Next

If this chapter feels uncomfortably familiar, that reaction makes sense.

It describes a failure mode many lawyers recognize but rarely name. The next chapter turns toward what happens when distorted time perception meets professional identity. Overcommitment does not arise from recklessness or ego. It grows out of optimism combined with time blindness.

Until that connection is addressed, the cycle will keep repeating.

Chapter 9
Overcommitment
Why Saying Yes Becomes a
Cognitive Survival Strategy

There is a moment that shows up before nearly every workload decision that later causes me trouble. It is not panic. It is not confusion. It is not even stress. It is confidence.

That is the part no one warns you about.

Overcommitment does not announce itself as a bad idea. It arrives quietly, dressed up as professionalism and good intentions. It feels like being capable. It feels like being needed. It feels like the calm belief that you can handle what is being asked of you because, historically, you always have.

In the practice of law, that feeling is rewarded early and often. Judges appreciate lawyers who step up. Clerks remember the ones who make problems go away. Clients cling to attorneys who say yes when others hesitate. Colleagues rely on the person who always seems willing to carry a little more weight. The system reinforces the idea that taking on more work is a sign of competence, not risk.

For a lawyer with ADHD, that reinforcement lands on fertile ground.

When I agree to something new, my brain does not immediately register cost. It does not run a careful inventory of time, energy, emotional bandwidth, or recovery. It does not calculate what else is already pending or what might go wrong between now and the deadline. Instead, it asks a simpler and far more dangerous question: could I do this if I had to?

The answer is usually yes.

That answer becomes the justification. It is technically true, which makes it persuasive. I have handled worse. I have pulled things together under tighter deadlines. I have survived heavier dockets. I have delivered results when the margin for error was thin. That history becomes evidence, and I mistake survival for sustainability.

Overcommitment begins there, not with chaos, but with optimism. It is the belief that future me will have more time, more clarity, and more discipline than present me does. It is the assumption that whatever is already on my plate will somehow take care of itself once the next obligation arrives. The problem is not that I do not care about the work. The problem is that my brain treats future obligations as abstract and distant, while the request in front of me feels immediate and real.

Legal practice makes this especially dangerous because nothing exists in isolation. One more case is never just one more case. One more continuance is never just a reset. One more deadline does not float independently. Everything stacks. Everything compounds. Everything eventually arrives at once.

By the time the pressure is obvious, the commitments are already made.

Overcommitment is not laziness. It is not arrogance. It is not a lack of boundaries in the way people usually mean that phrase. It is a failure to distinguish between what you are capable of doing and what you have the capacity to sustain. The legal profession rewards the former and ignores the latter, until the bill comes due.

This chapter is about how that happens, why it feels so reasonable when it does, and why good intentions, left unchecked, quietly turn into professional risk.

There are more ways overcommitment shows up in the life of a lawyer with ADHD than I can count. If you do not name it early and deal with it honestly, it takes a small, nagging problem and turns it into something bigger than it ever needed to be. It becomes exhaustion that follows you home. It becomes stress you cannot shake. It becomes sloppy work you never intended to produce. If the numbers get high enough and the pressure stays on long enough, it can even put you in the crosshairs of a disciplinary system that is not built to care why you fell behind. It only cares that you did.

One of the traps in law is that your reputation is both your foundation and your currency. People will forgive a lot if they believe you are competent, prepared, and straight with them. Clients trust you with their freedom, their money, and their lives. Judges trust you to show up ready and to move a case along without wasting the court's time. Clerks and court staff remember whether you are the lawyer who answers, the lawyer who follows through, the lawyer who can be counted on when the docket is clogged and everyone is tired. That good name is not vanity. It is a professional asset, and it takes years to build and one season of chaos to crack.

Overcommitment threatens that asset in a quiet way because it rarely announces itself as a problem at the start. It does not feel like incompetence when you agree to one more setting, one more hearing, one more "simple" motion, one more client meeting squeezed into an already full week. In the moment, it feels like professionalism. It feels like being the person who can handle things. It feels like being the lawyer the court can lean on. The cost is delayed. The consequences do not arrive until everything you promised shows up at the same time.

The volume is the danger. It is not that you are taking work you are not qualified to handle. It is that you are taking on more work than any one person can handle well, and you are doing it in a profession where "well" is not optional. The practice of law is not a hobby you can pick up and put down when your mood shifts. It is a system of deadlines, obligations, and consequences that does not care what else you had going on that week.

Continuances are one of the cleanest examples of how overcommitment grows without you noticing. Every time you agree to continue a case, you do not make the case go away. You extend it. You keep it alive in your calendar, in your mind, and in your client's life. The next time that matter comes around, it will not be the only one you are dealing with. That new setting lands on top of everything else you already had set, plus the new cases you took in the meantime, plus the emergencies that always seem to erupt at the worst possible moment. Then you look up and you are walking into court with a stack of files so thick it feels like a physical accusation.

In criminal cases, continuances also carry a consequence that has nothing to do with your comfort. If your client is incarcerated, every continuance is another stretch of time in a jail cell waiting for the system to get around to their case. Sometimes that delay is strategically necessary. Sometimes it is unavoidable. Still, it should never become casual. You should never forget that what feels like administrative breathing room to you can feel like punishment to a person sitting in a concrete box counting days. Overcommitment makes it easier to forget that because when you are overloaded, everything starts to look like a scheduling problem instead of a human problem.

Court appointed work adds another layer. Court appointments are some of the most meaningful cases you will ever take, and they can make you a better lawyer faster than anything else. They also come with their own pressure, especially if you are the kind of lawyer who ends up getting asked to take the cases no one else wants. There is a particular fear that creeps in, even if no one says it out loud. You worry that turning down an appointment will irritate the wrong person. You worry that you will be labeled difficult, unhelpful, not a team player. You worry that the next time you need grace on a crowded docket, it will not be there.

If you have ADHD, there is a second force working on you at the same time. Being needed can feel like fuel. It is a dopamine hit disguised as duty. The request itself can light you up. A clerk calls because they cannot find anyone else. A judge asks because the case is a mess and they want someone competent in the chair. Another lawyer asks because they are in trouble and they need help. In that moment, your brain does not run the full calculation. It hears urgency, importance, and validation, and it wants to say yes. That is how you become the person the system leans on while your own practice buckles.

Deadlines work the same way, and they might be even more dangerous because they can fool you into thinking they are far away. A deadline is never an isolated event. It exists alongside court settings, client demands, jail visits, hearings, motion practice, and the normal interruptions of life. In a practice like criminal defense, you can also have trials drop onto the calendar in a way that collapses the month you thought you had. The problem is not that you do not understand deadlines intellectually. The problem is that an ADHD brain tends to experience time differently. There is now and not now. There is what is urgent and what is invisible. A deadline thirty days away can feel like it does not exist until it is close enough to cause pain.

That is how a thirty-day brief becomes due in thirty minutes. You are not lazy. You are not indifferent. You are operating with a time sense that collapses the future into a vague blur until the moment arrives and the pressure becomes real. Overcommitment makes that collapse more likely because it strips away margin. It leaves no room to start early, no room to revise, no room for the inevitable day when you wake up and your brain will not cooperate. When there is no margin, you end up living in an emergency mindset.

Criminal practice already carries urgency. Judges ask questions and want answers on the spot. Clients call from jail in a panic. Witnesses disappear. Discovery arrives late. Dockets change without warning. It is hectic work even when your caseload is reasonable. Overcommitment takes that baseline urgency and turns it into a lifestyle. You start triaging instead of practicing. You start reacting instead of planning. You start running your office the way you might run a fire scene, handling whatever is smoking the most in the moment and hoping nothing else catches.

This is where having a plan matters. A real plan. Not a vague intention to do better next month. Every practice needs a caseload ceiling, and you have to decide what yours is while you are calm, not while you are cornered. You have to know how many cases you can handle without losing the ability to think, to prepare, to return calls, to file motions on time, to show up in court with the file actually read and understood. If you do not set that number, the system will set it for you, and the number will be higher than your brain can sustain.

If there is one lesson overcommitment eventually teaches, it is this: you cannot rely on your internal sense of capacity. That sense is unreliable, especially when you are calm, confident, and not yet under pressure. The danger is not that you do not work hard enough. The danger is that you consistently believe you will be able to work harder later.

Containment begins with accepting that truth without moral judgment. This is not about self-control or grit. It is about recognizing that your brain does not forecast workload accurately, and then building rules that operate when your instincts cannot be trusted.

For me, containment starts with a plan for my caseload that exists before anyone asks me for anything. Not a loose goal. Not a vague hope. A number. A range. A line I do not cross without deliberate thought. When I am calm, when nothing is on fire, when I am not standing in a hallway being asked to "just take one more," that is when the rules get made. Those rules are not negotiable in the moment because the moment is exactly when I make bad decisions.

Part of containment is friction. If saying yes is easy, you will say yes. So the system has to slow you down. I learned to give myself time before agreeing to new work, even when the answer was likely to be yes. I stopped answering commitment questions immediately. I learned to say, "Let me look at my calendar," even when I already knew what it said. That pause is not avoidance. It is protection. It creates space between the request and the decision, and in that space, I am far more likely to choose correctly.

Containment also means deciding in advance what kinds of work I will and will not take, and under what conditions. Not every case deserves the same level of intensity. Not every client needs a trial. Some matters are destined for resolution early, and others are going to demand everything you have. When I fail to make those distinctions up front, everything becomes urgent and nothing gets done well. A plan allows me to allocate energy instead of reacting to chaos.

This is especially true with appointed work. There is real pressure there, and it is not imagined. Judges remember who helps. Clerks remember who says yes. Courts rely on the lawyers who step in when no one else will. Being needed feels good. It provides a rush of relevance and approval that can override better judgment. Containment requires acknowledging that pull without pretending it does not exist. It means reminding yourself that professionalism includes sustainability, and that taking every case today may cost you your ability to practice tomorrow.

Deadlines require containment too. A deadline is never just a date on a calendar. It is work that competes with every other obligation you already have. When you treat deadlines as isolated events, you underestimate their cumulative effect. I learned that agreeing to continuances, resetting hearings, or pushing briefing deadlines forward does not create breathing room. It shifts pressure into the future, where it multiplies. Containment means treating future time as real and limited, not abstract and forgiving.

The common thread here is simple but uncomfortable. You do not rise to the level of your intentions. You fall to the level of your systems. Containment is the system that keeps good intentions from becoming professional liabilities. It does not make you less capable. It makes your capability usable.

Once you accept that, the question stops being whether you could take on more. The question becomes whether you should. And that is a far safer question for a lawyer to answer.

Containment is where responsibility actually lives. Not responsibility as punishment or guilt, but responsibility as stewardship. If you do not decide in advance how much you can carry, the system will decide for you. Courts will keep setting dates. Clients will keep asking for more. Colleagues will keep assuming you are available. None of that happens because you are weak or disorganized. It happens because you are competent, responsive, and willing. Those qualities are admirable. They are also dangerous if left unbounded.

What containment does is create a perimeter around your practice before you are tired, behind, or emotionally compromised. It gives you something to point to when you are asked to take on more than you should. A plan. A rule. A line you did not invent in the moment to make someone else feel better. When you decide your limits while calm, you are protecting future-you from making promises under pressure. You are not shrinking your practice. You are making it survivable.

But containment alone does not explain why so many of us step past those limits anyway. Even with a plan. Even with rules. Even with experience. There is another force at work, quieter and more personal, that pushes us to override our own safeguards. It is the reflex to smooth things over. To avoid disappointing someone. To say yes when no would be safer. To absorb discomfort rather than hand it back to the person who created it.

That force is not ambition. It is not generosity. It is not professionalism. It is people pleasing. And until you understand how it operates in the ADHD nervous system, every containment strategy you build will be tested at its weakest point: the moment someone needs you, asks you, or expects you to say yes.

One of the most useful discipline tools I ever adopted did not come from a productivity book, a CLE, or a practice-management consultant. It came from the simple realization that not every case deserves the same kind of attention, and pretending otherwise is one of the fastest ways to overload yourself.

Early on, I treated every new case as if it were headed for trial. I did this partly out of instinct and partly out of fear. Trial work is where lawyers earn their reputations, and it is also where ADHD brains tend to feel most alive. When everything is framed as a potential fight, the work feels urgent, meaningful, and important. The problem is that most cases are not going to trial, and treating them as if they are creates a false sense of future obligation that never goes away.

At some point, I learned to make a quiet decision early. Not a public declaration, not a promise to a client, and not a concession to the State. Just an internal classification. Is this a case that is likely to resolve, or is this a case that is likely to be fought? That single question changed how I carried the case in my head.

Cases that are going to resolve still deserve care. They still require preparation, judgment, and attention. But they do not require the same long-term mental bandwidth as cases that are headed toward a jury. They do not need to live rent-free in your mind every waking hour. They do not need to be rehearsed endlessly in your head while you are driving, showering, or trying to sleep.

Cases that are going to trial are different. They demand space. They demand planning. They demand that you protect time around them instead of stacking more and more obligations on top. When you fail to distinguish between these two categories, everything feels like a trial case, and your calendar slowly becomes a work of fiction.

Overcommitment thrives on that fiction. If every case feels equally urgent and equally demanding, your brain never gets relief. There is no sense of progress, only the constant feeling that something important is being neglected. That feeling feeds anxiety, procrastination, and eventually avoidance. It also feeds the temptation to keep saying yes, because nothing feels finished anyway.

This kind of early triage is not about pessimism or lack of commitment. It is about honesty. Lawyers make these judgments every day whether they admit it or not. The danger for a lawyer with ADHD is not making the judgment. The danger is refusing to make it consciously and letting every case occupy the same mental space.

Once I started doing this, something subtle changed. My schedule became more realistic. My stress became more predictable. I stopped borrowing time from the future without realizing it. I still worked hard, but I worked with intention instead of panic.

Overcommitment is not cured by working faster or caring less. It is managed by deciding, early and deliberately, where your energy actually belongs.

Sticking to a plan is hard when you have ADHD because you can talk yourself into anything. You can always imagine that future you will have more time, more energy, more focus. You can always believe that this one extra case will not matter. It will. It always does, because there is no such thing as one extra obligation in a profession built on accumulation. The moment you break your own boundary, you train yourself that the boundary was never real.

A plan does not make you selfish. It makes you professional. We are not volunteers wandering through a courthouse hoping someone will approve of us. We are trained professionals, and we control our practices or we pay the price. That does not mean you stop caring. It means you stop confusing care with surrender. It means you protect your bandwidth so your clients get the version of you they hired or were appointed to receive, not the burnt-out version operating on fumes and adrenaline.

Overcommitment looks good right up until it does not. It can make you seem dependable until the day it makes you late. It can make you seem generous until the day it makes you resentful. It can make you seem invincible until the day you wake up, look at your calendar, and realize there is no possible way to be in six courtrooms, handle twenty cases, return every call, draft every motion, and still function like a competent adult.

The solution is not shame. The solution is structure. Name your limits while you still have the power to enforce them. Decide what your practice is and what it is not. Decide what you will take and what you will refer out. Decide how many active cases you can carry before the quality starts to slip. Then protect that plan like it is part of your license, because in a very real way, it is.

If overcommitment were only a planning problem, this chapter would end with containment and move on. Caseload caps. Pre-decided rules. Friction against yes. Decisions made while calm. On paper, that should be enough. For a lot of lawyers, it is.

For lawyers with ADHD, it often is not.

This is the part that took me years to understand. I could build a rational system for my practice and still violate it in a single conversation. Not because the system was flawed. Because something stronger than planning stepped in.

People.

A judge asking for help.

A clerk needing a favor.

A colleague looking relieved when I said yes.

A client whose voice cracked on the phone.

That is where containment goes to die. Overcommitment is the cognitive mistake. People pleasing is the emotional override. When the two combine, even well-designed systems start to leak. The rules still exist, but they lose authority in the moment. The plan becomes theoretical, and the relationship in front of you becomes real.

This is not about being weak. It is about being wired to experience social friction as threat. Saying no does not feel like a neutral business decision. It feels like rejection, conflict, disappointment, or abandonment. In that moment, your brain is not solving a scheduling problem. It is trying to keep the room calm.

So you make exceptions. Just this once.

Just for this judge. Just for this case. Just because you can handle it.

And because you are competent, because you have pulled off worse before, because you do not feel overwhelmed yet, the yes feels justified. The system bends. Then it bends again. Then it collapses quietly, weeks later, when the calendar fills and the margin disappears.

This is why overcommitment cannot be solved by planning alone. It requires an honest look at the emotional forces that defeat planning at the exact moment it matters most. That force has a name.

People pleasing.

There is a difference between what you are capable of doing and what you have the capacity to sustain. That difference is where most ADHD lawyers get hurt.

Capability is seductive. It is visible. It is provable. You can point to it. You have tried cases you should not have won. You have written motions under impossible deadlines. You have pulled coherence out of chaos more times than you can count. When someone asks whether you can handle something, capability answers immediately. Yes, I can do that. I have done harder things than this.

Capacity is quieter. It does not announce itself. It does not show up in a crisis. It reveals itself over time, in patterns, in wear, in the slow erosion of margin. Capacity asks different questions. How much can I carry without dropping something else. How long can I operate at this level before the cracks start to show. What does this cost me tomorrow, not just tonight.

The legal profession rewards capability and ignores capacity. It is structured to notice who shows up, who delivers, who saves the day. It does not ask how many hours that cost you, what you postponed to make it happen, or how many future problems you created by pulling it off this time. For a lawyer with ADHD, that imbalance is dangerous, because capability is the one thing we have always been able to access under pressure.

This is where overcommitment takes root. When you say yes, you are not lying. You are not exaggerating. You really can do the thing you are agreeing to do. The mistake is assuming that because you can do it, you should. Or worse, assuming that doing it once means you can do it repeatedly without consequence.

Capacity is not about talent. It is about throughput. It is about how many matters you can hold in your head without losing track of deadlines. It is about how many emotionally charged clients you can manage without burning out. It is about how many promises you can make before one of them becomes impossible to keep.

ADHD complicates this because time does not register the way it does for other people. Future obligations feel abstract. They exist somewhere out there, disconnected from the present moment. When you agree to take something on, you are not experiencing the full weight of that commitment. You are experiencing the idea of it, stripped of friction, stripped of fatigue, stripped of everything that will make it hard when it finally arrives.

That is why the collision is always delayed. Nothing goes wrong at the moment you overcommit. The trouble comes later, when all the reasonable decisions converge at once. When the cases you agreed to in isolation show up together. When the deadlines you spaced out in your mind stack on top of each other in reality. When the system demands performance at the same time your capacity is already exhausted.

Overcommitment, on its own, would already be enough to derail a practice. Too many cases. Too many deadlines. Too little margin. But overcommitment rarely exists in isolation, especially in the legal profession.

Once you are stretched thin, a second force steps in and keeps the damage going.

People start to notice that you are reliable. Judges notice. Clerks notice. Colleagues notice. Clients notice. You are the lawyer who answers the phone. The lawyer who steps up. The lawyer who does not complain. The lawyer who finds a way.

And that recognition feels good. It quiets anxiety. It creates relief. It provides a hit of reassurance in a profession that traffics in judgment and evaluation. Saying yes does not just manage workload. It manages fear.

At that point, the problem is no longer just time or capacity. It becomes relational. Saying no feels like risk. Disappointing someone feels dangerous. Letting someone down feels like exposure.

So the yeses keep coming, even when you know better. Even when your calendar is full. Even when your body is tired. Even when your judgment is starting to fray.

This is not weakness. It is conditioning.

Once overcommitment is socially rewarded, people pleasing takes over as the mechanism that sustains it. And by the time you realize what is happening, the system has already learned something important about you. It has learned that you will absorb the pressure.

Chapter 10
The People Pleasing Attorney
Why Lawyers With ADHD Say Yes
When They Should Say No

There is a specific kind of person the legal profession quietly depends on but almost never understands. It is the person who cannot tolerate the idea of letting someone down. The person who takes the late-night call, agrees to the impossible deadline, rearranges a docket without complaint, apologizes reflexively, and turns discomfort into productivity.

From the outside, this behavior is praised. Judges call it professionalism. Colleagues call it being a team player. Clients call it dedication. Entire offices function because someone like this is always willing to absorb the pressure and keep things moving.

Inside the mind of a person with ADHD, however, people pleasing is something else entirely. It is not generosity. It is not kindness. It is not emotional intelligence. It is self-preservation.

It is survival. And it is one of the most dangerous behavioral patterns an ADHD-wired lawyer can develop, because the legal system will test it relentlessly, clients will drain it without noticing, courts will reward it in the short term, and disciplinary bodies will punish the inevitable collapse that follows.

No one warns you about that part.

Why ADHD Brains Default to People Pleasing

When most lawyers say they do not want to disappoint someone, they are describing a preference. They would rather avoid discomfort, but they can tolerate it when necessary. When a lawyer with ADHD says the same thing, they are describing a threat response.

Rejection Sensitivity Dysphoria sits underneath this behavior. It is not simply disliking criticism. It is an acute emotional reaction to perceived rejection, disappointment, or disapproval that lands with physical force. A pause on the phone, a clipped email, a raised eyebrow from the bench can register as danger.

The legal profession is saturated with judgment. Every filing is evaluated. Every argument is weighed. Every appearance invites scrutiny. For a person with ADHD, that environment creates a second, invisible trial that runs alongside the official one.

People pleasing becomes a form of armor. If everyone is satisfied, no one is disappointed. If no one is disappointed, the internal pressure eases. Saying yes quiets the noise, at least temporarily.

So yes becomes automatic. Yes to the extra case. Yes to the rushed deadline. Yes to the emotional labor. Yes to the thing you already know you cannot sustain. The mind understands the risk, but the nervous system demands relief.

The irony is hard to ignore. The same person who can dismantle an opposing case under pressure can unravel when a client sounds unhappy. The courtroom is manageable. Disappointment is not.

The Cost of Keeping the Peace

On paper, people pleasing looks harmless. A cooperative lawyer rarely draws attention for the wrong reasons. Over time, though, the cost accumulates quietly.

It shows up in the cases that should have been declined but were not. It shows up in deadlines accepted without margin. It shows up in promises made to calm anxiety rather than reflect reality. It shows up in the emotional weight carried home after every conversation.

Each accommodation drains executive function. Each concession narrows the margin for error. The work does not stop when the file is closed, because the emotional residue lingers long after.

People often misunderstand ADHD as a problem of distraction. In practice, the greater danger is overload. The mind is constantly triaging emotional signals, prioritizing perceived threats, and managing the reactions of others. The actual legal work competes with that internal labor for attention.

From the outside, everything looks calm. Inside, it feels like treading water with weights strapped to your ankles.

I did not recognize people pleasing as a pattern until long after I had internalized it as professionalism.

The setting was familiar. A routine criminal matter, nothing novel on the law, nothing dramatic in the posture. The client wanted movement. The court wanted efficiency. The prosecutor wanted resolution. I wanted to be seen as prepared, reasonable, and cooperative. Those are not bad instincts in criminal defense. They are often necessary.

The moment that sticks with me happened outside the courtroom, in a hallway conversation that never appears in any transcript. The judge asked whether the case could be set for a motions hearing. I had received discovery. I had begun reviewing it. I knew additional time would allow for deeper preparation, but I also knew the request was not unreasonable. I made a judgment call and agreed to the setting.

At the time, that decision felt appropriate. It was consistent with how cases moved. It avoided unnecessary delay. It respected the court's schedule. No one objected. My client expressed confidence. Nothing about the exchange felt improper or risky.

What I did not appreciate then was how easily those decisions stack.

Once I agreed to that first setting, the pace of the case was effectively set by the court's calendar rather than by my own assessment of preparation needs. Subsequent scheduling decisions followed that same rhythm. None of them, standing alone, crossed a line. Each one was defensible. Each one was made in good faith. The cumulative effect, however, was a narrowing of margin.

In criminal defense, margin matters.

By the time the motions hearing arrived, I was prepared. I had reviewed the file. I had outlined arguments. I had anticipated responses. The hearing went as expected. The court was attentive. The prosecutor responded. The record was made. Nothing went wrong.

What I noticed, though, was internal. I knew I could have done more with additional time. Not because I had failed to prepare, but because the preparation had been compressed. The difference was subtle, but it was there. It showed up not as a mistake, but as missed opportunity.

After the hearing, my client asked whether the issue could have been pushed further. I explained where we were procedurally and what came next. That explanation was accurate. What I did not say out loud was that earlier decisions had limited how much pressure could be applied at that stage.

This pattern repeated itself in other cases. Agreeing to settings that were feasible but tight. Taking calls later in the day than necessary to reassure clients. Responding quickly to avoid appearing unresponsive. None of this felt like overextension at the time. It felt like diligence.

People pleasing in criminal defense practice usually comes across as reliability more than weakness. Judges notice lawyers who do not create friction. Clerks remember attorneys who accommodate scheduling problems. Clients appreciate responsiveness. Prosecutors assume cooperation will continue.

Each of those reactions reinforces the behavior. The lawyer who says yes becomes the lawyer the system leans on.

The difficulty is that the system starts to track compliance without ever tracking cost. Over time, I began to notice that my most stressful weeks were not driven by the complexity of the cases themselves. They were driven by volume and compression. Too many reasonable commitments clustered together. Too little space between obligations. The stress did not come from the work. It came from the calendar.

That was the point where I began to understand people pleasing not as a personality trait, but as a professional risk factor.

The instinct to smooth interactions, to reduce tension, to keep everyone comfortable in the moment is understandable in a courtroom environment. Conflict carries consequences. Reputation matters. No one wants to be labeled difficult. For someone wired to experience interpersonal friction as heightened stress, the pull toward accommodation is strong.

The problem is that criminal defense is not a service industry built on comfort. It is an adversarial process built on timing, leverage, and preparation. When decisions are made primarily to keep the room calm, those elements can erode quietly.

What changed for me was not a dramatic event or a single bad outcome. It was the recognition that professionalism includes restraint. Saying not yet, or I need additional time, or this schedule does not work is not a failure to cooperate. It is part of competent representation.

Judges are accustomed to lawyers who ask for time when they need it. Prosecutors adjust. Clients adapt. The fear that everything will collapse if you introduce friction is often exaggerated by your own nervous system.

People pleasing taught me that good intentions are not a substitute for deliberate decision making. It also taught me that avoiding short term discomfort can create long term strain. Once I understood that, I became more careful about when and why I said yes. Not to protect my image, but to protect my practice. The work improved. The stress decreased. The calendar became something I controlled rather than something that controlled me.

That lesson can make you more effective rather than less professional.

Why This Trait Often Produces Excellent Trial Work

There is a reason people pleasing persists. In controlled environments, it can be an advantage.

Sensitivity to emotional shifts translates into an ability to read rooms quickly. Subtle changes in tone, posture, and expression do not go unnoticed. That awareness allows for rapid adjustment. Arguments shift. Cadence changes. Pressure points are identified before others recognize them.

This is not mystical intuition. It is hypervigilance refined through experience. Years of scanning for emotional cues sharpen perception in ways that are difficult to teach.

In trial settings, that awareness can be decisive. Jurors respond to it. Judges react to it. Witnesses reveal more than they intend. The skill is real, and it is rewarded.

The problem is that the same sensitivity does not switch off outside the courtroom. The radar stays active. Clients, colleagues, and administrators are all treated as potential emotional hazards. Saying no feels reckless, even when it is necessary.

Empathy, without boundaries, turns inward and becomes self-destructive.

How People Pleasing Becomes a Discipline Problem

People pleasing itself does not violate any rule. The consequences it produces often do.

Overpromising leads to missed deadlines. Avoiding conflict delays hard conversations. Absorbing responsibility crowds out preparation. Time intended for writing is spent managing emotions instead.

When something finally slips, the system responds to the surface behavior. A deadline is missed. A call goes unanswered. A filing is late. The analysis rarely goes further.

Disciplinary bodies measure conduct. They do not measure fear. They do not examine the internal calculations that led to the failure. They see outcomes, not process.

For lawyers with ADHD, people pleasing is often the invisible mechanism beneath conduct that later appears negligent. The profession treats the result as a moral lapse rather than a predictable consequence of unmanaged neurological stress.

The Internal Logic That Drives the Behavior

What is often misunderstood is that people pleasing is not about approval. It is about avoidance.

The internal dialogue rarely sounds dramatic. It is quiet and relentless. If I say no, this will escalate. If it escalates, I will be judged. If I am judged, my competence will be questioned. If my competence is questioned, everything I have built is at risk.

Saying yes interrupts that chain. It feels safer in the moment, even when the cost is deferred.

For someone without ADHD, boundaries are decisions. For someone with ADHD, boundaries are protective structures that prevent collapse. Without them, the nervous system defaults to the path of least immediate pain.

Why Boundaries Are Not Optional

This is the pivot point. Motivation is not the solution. Insight is not enough.

Boundaries function as accommodations. They reduce exposure to situations that trigger maladaptive responses. They preserve executive function for work that actually requires it.

A boundary does not need to be dramatic. It needs to be firm. It needs to be predictable. It needs to exist before pressure arrives.

Limiting availability, narrowing intake, controlling communication channels, and refusing to commit on the spot are not preferences. They are safeguards.

Without them, people pleasing will continue to erode performance until something breaks.

Naming the Pattern Without Shame

People pleasing is not a character flaw. It is not immaturity. It is not weakness.

It is a behavioral adaptation developed by an ADHD nervous system in an environment that constantly applies pressure. It works until it does not.

Left unexamined, it quietly undermines careers. When understood and structured, it can be redirected into effective advocacy without self-destruction.

The profession benefits from this trait far more than it admits. It also bears responsibility for the damage it causes when left unchecked.

Recognizing people pleasing for what it is does not excuse failures. It explains them. And explanation is the first step toward designing systems that prevent the failures from occurring again.

People pleasing is often described as a relational problem, a difficulty with boundaries or conflict. In practice, it is something heavier and more corrosive. Every accommodation carries cognitive cost. Every softened response requires regulation. Every decision to absorb tension rather than surface it draws from a reserve that is rarely acknowledged and never replenished. Over time, that quiet work accumulates. The lawyer continues to function, continues to appear reliable, continues to hold the room together, while the internal load grows denser and harder to carry. What makes this dangerous is not the individual act of accommodation, but the fact that the labor remains unseen, even by the person performing it. That is where the real cost begins to accrue.

Chapter 11
The Activation Barrier
Initiation Failure in Low-Urgency Systems

If you read enough productivity books, you start to think you're broken. They all say the same thing, just with different covers: "Decide to start, then begin."

That sentence looks clean on paper. In the real world, especially the legal world, that sentence might as well be written in Sanskrit. People with ADHD don't struggle because the task is difficult. We struggle because beginning is a uphill, neurological fistfight.

Starting is not a moral decision. It is a dopamine event.

Let's talk about dopamine. Not in a textbook, brain-scan, double-blind study kind of way. Let's talk about it the way someone with ADHD *lives it.*

Dopamine is the chemical that tells your brain "this matters." It's the spark. The starter fluid. The gas pedal. Neurotypical brains have a steady, predictable drip of dopamine that flows into the frontal lobe, the part of the brain where decisions get made, plans become action, and thoughts line up in some kind of logical sequence. They get a signal when something is important, and they can act on it.

People with ADHD don't get that steady drip. We get a low idle. A quiet engine. Nothing at the wheel. We know what needs to be done, we see the work sitting right there in front of us, but there's no ignition. No spark. No "go." It's like trying to start a car with no fuel in the tank. The battery is fine. The tires are good. The engine is capable. But without gas, the car just sits there.

That's task paralysis in one sentence.

If you are a lawyer with ADHD, there will come a point in your career when a moment like this lands hard enough that you remember it years later. If you do not recognize it yet, you will. And if you think you never will, you probably just have not noticed it happening.

There was a judge I appeared before regularly for years. Outstanding in every respect. Careful. Fair. Thorough. The kind of judge who reads what you file and expects you to have done the same. Not out of ego, but out of respect for the process. If the law required work, she expected the work to be done. I respected her deeply.

I tried cases in her courtroom and won. I argued motions successfully. I represented clients well, and the outcomes reflected that. And like any lawyer who practices long enough in one place, there were moments where I fell short—not in outcome, but in execution.

In one case, the court invited briefing on an issue that mattered. It was not a rebuke. It was not a sanction. It was an opportunity to shape the analysis.

And I froze.

Task paralysis does not announce itself as refusal. It does not feel like defiance. It feels like standing still while knowing exactly what needs to be done and being unable to make the first move. The brief never came together. Not because the issue was hard. Not because I did not care. But because starting never happened.

As it turned out, neither side submitted briefing, and the court resolved the issue without it. The ruling favored my client. There was no harm. No fallout. On paper, nothing went wrong. However, something shifted for me.

For a while afterward, every time I stood in that courtroom, I felt it. A sense of having disappointed someone whose respect mattered to me. Whether that disappointment was real or imagined is something I still cannot say with certainty. It may have lived entirely inside my own head. But it lived there vividly.

I replayed it over and over. Not the missed filing itself, but the feeling that I had let something slip that should not have slipped. That I had not shown up as the lawyer I knew I could be. That I had failed to meet a standard I cared about, even when the outcome said otherwise.

What stayed with me was not guilt over the brief. It was grief over the inability to write it.

That distinction matters. It matters because this was not about laziness or neglect. It was about a neurological failure of ignition. About knowing exactly what to do and being unable to start. About carrying the weight of that inability into every subsequent appearance, every interaction, every moment where professionalism and self-worth quietly collide.

That is the cost of the activation barrier when it goes unrecognized. The system moves on. The docket clears. The case resolves. The lawyer carries it.

That moment stayed with me because it clarified something I had been misunderstanding for years. The damage was never in the outcome. The case resolved. The client was fine. The system moved on. The damage was internal, quiet, and cumulative. It lived in the space between knowing what I was capable of and being unable, in that moment, to access it. That is the cost of an activation barrier the profession does not see and lawyers are trained not to name. Until that barrier is understood for what it is, these moments will keep being misread as lapses instead of signals. And lawyers with ADHD will keep carrying weight that never makes it onto the record.

Dopamine is not about pleasure. People think it's the "feel good" chemical. Wrong. It's the anticipation chemical. It's the drive, the craving, the *wanting*. Dopamine is the voice saying, "Let's do this." Without dopamine, nothing feels compelling. Nothing feels urgent. Even the things that are urgent — filing a motion, answering discovery, making a phone call that has to be made before close of business — don't light up the board. The ADHD brain sees the task but does not *feel* it.

And that's the problem: ADHD is not a disorder of knowing. It's a disorder of doing. Now flip the switch.

When dopamine finally spikes — when something is interesting, risky, novel, unpredictable — suddenly the whole system roars to life. Lawyers with ADHD know exactly what I mean. Trial does that. The rush of cross-examination, the tightrope of objection practice, the adrenaline of twelve people watching your every word. Dopamine lights every bulb on the board.

That's why people with ADHD can hyperfocus like snipers. Total clarity. Tunnel vision. Hours pass like minutes. And that's why people with ADHD chase dopamine like a second heartbeat. We're not thrill seekers. We're trying to get our brains to turn on.

Dopamine is the difference between staring at the blank caption of a motion for an hour and writing ten pages in thirty minutes when something finally clicks. It's not weakness. It's wiring.

You don't "try harder" to make dopamine. You engineer situations to trigger it, urgency, novelty, deadlines, movement, stakes. Once you understand that, ADHD stops looking like laziness and starts looking like what it always was: A brain built for ignition, not routine.

If you don't have enough internal activation to make a task feel meaningful, it doesn't matter how much you plan, intend, promise, or panic — nothing happens. You sit. You stare. You know exactly what needs to be done and you can't make yourself do it.

And here's the worst part: you look perfectly capable from the outside. To the world, you look like someone choosing not to start. Inside, it feels like someone welded your feet to the floor.

That state has a name. It is task paralysis.

This chapter is not about discipline, and it is not about motivation. Those concepts assume an engine that is already running. This chapter is about lowering the ignition point so the engine actually starts. Not finishing.

Starting.

There was a motion I needed to file that should have taken so little time at all.

Not a novel issue. Not a risky argument. Just a routine filing that I had written dozens of times before. The law was settled. The facts were straightforward. Nothing about it required creativity or brilliance.

I sat down at my desk fully intending to knock it out and move on.

The file was open. The deadline was reasonable. The stakes were real, but not dramatic. This was the kind of work lawyers tell themselves they'll "clean up" between bigger things.

And I couldn't start.

I stared at the screen longer than I care to admit. Not blankly. Actively. Thinking. Reviewing. Re-reviewing. Mentally rehearsing how I would structure it. Where I would save it. Which prior version I should pull. Whether I had used this argument most recently in a different case. Whether the local rule had changed since the last time.

None of those questions were urgent. All of them were unanswered. So I drifted.

Not intentionally. Not irresponsibly. My attention slid sideways into something adjacent, an old email thread, a case I remembered arguing, a procedural issue that suddenly felt more interesting than the task in front of me.

That is task paralysis.

And once you see it for what it is, you stop asking why you "can't just start," and start asking a much more useful question:

"How do I make starting unavoidable?"

The brain doesn't freeze on difficulty; it freezes on decisions.

One of the most persistent misunderstandings about ADHD is the belief that paralysis happens because the work is too hard.

That has never been true for me.

Hard work has never scared me. Complexity has never scared me. I went to law school. I try cases. I argue motions that matter to people whose lives are on the line. Difficulty is not the problem. If anything, difficulty tends to sharpen me.

What stops me is uncertainty.

When my brain locks up, it is almost never because I don't know how to do the work. It is because I cannot see the beginning clearly enough to step into it. The task itself may be familiar. The law may be settled. The outcome may even be predictable. But if the starting point is fuzzy, my brain refuses to move.

Internally, the experience is not panic or avoidance. It is interrogation.

My brain does not say, "I can't write this motion." It says, "Where does this motion live?"

"Which version did I use last time?"

"What did I call the file?"

"Is there a procedural step I'm forgetting that will come back to hurt me?"

"Am I about to do this wrong in a way I won't discover until it's too late?"

None of those questions are irrational. In fact, every one of them reflects professional caution. They are the kinds of questions competent lawyers are supposed to ask. The problem is not the questions themselves. The problem is that they all arrive at once, before a single word has been written.

That is executive function strain.

Each unresolved decision adds friction at the exact moment movement is required. For a neurotypical brain, that friction is tolerable. For an ADHD brain, it is often fatal to initiation. The system stalls before the engine ever turns over.

This is why advice like "just start" misses the point entirely.

Starting is not a moral choice. It is not a motivational breakthrough. It is a mechanical event that depends on how many decisions the brain has to hold at the threshold. When that number exceeds a certain point, the brain does not argue or negotiate. It freezes.

From the outside, this looks like delay.

From the inside, it feels like standing in front of a door that should open, except there is no handle and no sign explaining how it works.

This is also why ADHD paralysis is so often misread as laziness or procrastination. Observers see inactivity and assume unwillingness. They do not see the internal bottleneck created by too many simultaneous variables competing for resolution before action is permitted.

Once the first step becomes obvious, everything changes. If the starting line is visible, I can move. If the task has a clear entry point, I can engage. If the beginning requires no strategic decisions, my brain will step forward willingly.

After that, I can handle almost anything.

The work does not need to be easy. It can be complex, demanding, and intellectually heavy. What it cannot be is undefined at the point of ignition. Ambiguity at the starting line is the one thing my brain consistently cannot tolerate.

That is why lowering the activation barrier matters.

It is not about making the work smaller or less serious. It is about stripping unnecessary decisions out of the beginning so the brain can enter the task without resistance. Once the engine turns over, momentum does the rest.

The tragedy is that many lawyers with ADHD internalize this freeze as a personal failure. They assume the problem is discipline, willpower, or professionalism. They push harder, shame themselves, and promise to do better next time—without ever addressing the actual mechanism that caused the stall.

The work was never the problem. The friction existed in the number of decisions between intention and action.

Lowering the activation barrier is a form of neuro-engineering.

Here's something I learned way too late: I don't need easier work. I need easier beginnings. There's a difference. The work can be hard. I can handle hard.

What I can't handle is unclear and unstarted. So I started building systems where tasks begin before I think about them.

Like this:

- Desktop folder: "Motion Templates - USE FIRST"
- Separate document just for captions
- A legal pad that literally says: "WRITE ONE SENTENCE."

It was nothing fancy. Nothing sexy. Just externalizing the parts my brain cannot hold. My dopamine doesn't respond to a blank page. It responds to progress.

Even fake progress works. One line. One header. One saved filename. That's ignition.

The Bond Motion That Went Sideways

In criminal practice, bond reduction motions are supposed to be routine. They're not glamorous, they're not dramatic, but they matter — sometimes more than anything else I do. Tennessee law guarantees that a person charged with a crime has the right to bond. The Constitution says it, judges know it, and prosecutors will even nod along when you say it in open court.

But there's a nasty little secret tucked behind that constitutional promise:

Having bond and being able to make bond are two very different things.

I had a client once — three separate indictments hanging over his head, all filed in the same general timeframe. Each case came with its own bond. Stack them together and the number was more than his family could ever dream of posting. I was sitting in my office talking through strategy with my investigator, trying to figure out the global picture so we could put a reasonable reduction in front of the court.

She turned to her computer and started looking it up on the clerk's website. Three minutes. That's all it took. Just a simple search while I stared off at whatever I had been doing before she came in.

Then she turned back to me and said, "Okay, Michael. Total is $85,000. They broke it down — first case is twenty, second is forty-five, third is twenty."

I looked up, confused, as if she had suddenly started speaking Portuguese.

"What are you talking about?"

She gave me that look — a mix of surprise and disbelief — because she had just spent the last five minutes standing there with me discussing the exact same client, the exact same issue. She said, "David's bond motion. You wanted the totals."

"Oh," I said, like someone waking up in the wrong house, "right."

Then I did something that still makes me shake my head. I simply closed my laptop screen. And in that moment I realized I had been working — but not on the bond motion, not on my client's freedom, not on anything remotely connected to his case.

I had drifted.

In the span of three minutes I had slid from a critical legal task — a task that could mean the difference between a jury trial and a guilty plea — into something completely unrelated. Something absurd. I don't even remember what it was that day, but I know the pattern too well:

One minute I'm advocating for a man's liberty, and the next minute I'm reading about polishing leather shoes, or vintage Rolex movements, or whether English or Italian tailoring produces a sharper lapel.

That's ADHD. Not laziness. Not indifference. A sudden, unplanned migration of attention toward whatever grabbed the dopamine first.

The courtroom is easy for me because urgency is baked in. Evidence, objections, eye contact with jurors — the dopamine writes its own script. But sitting alone in a quiet office, staring at a blank caption page on a bond motion?

The urgency isn't there. The fire isn't lit. And the focus wanders.

My investigator thought I was zoning out. Truth is, I was in hyper-focus, just on the wrong thing at the wrong time. That's the irony:

I can go all-in. I just don't get to choose where "in" goes.

Drafting a bond motion is straightforward: title, docket numbers, statutory basis, circumstances, ties to the community, ability to pay. Twenty minutes of work. But ADHD doesn't care about "straightforward." It cares about stimulation.

This moment wasn't catastrophic. I filed the motion. We got the reduction. But it was a warning sign, and one repeated hundreds of times throughout my career.

For lawyers with ADHD, effort is rarely absent; it is often misallocated.

Activation Through Music

I didn't believe in "8D audio" when I first heard it. It sounded like one of those Internet gimmicks, "listen with headphones, it'll change your life." But then I put it on. And something happened that I can't deny: my brain quieted down just enough for me to start working.

Here's what 8D audio really is. It's not a different dimension of music. It's stereo sound that's been engineered to move, slowly, continuously, around your head. Instead of music blasting from a flat point directly into your ears, the sound shifts left to right, front to back, like someone is circling you with a speaker. Some tracks even simulate distance. Near. Far. Behind. Above.

To a neurotypical brain, this is a novelty. But to the ADHD brain, it's regulation.

ADHD isn't a deficit of attention. It's a deficit of *controlled* attention. The ADHD nervous system is constantly looking for dopamine, novelty, and movement, anything that feels alive enough to get through the static. That's why silence is so brutal for us. Silence doesn't equate to calm. Silence is threat detection. Silence is the brain asking a thousand questions at once and answering none of them.

8D audio is structured stimulation. It gives the ADHD brain something to track, but something simple. The mind says, "Where's the sound now?" and that tiny, continuous shift becomes a single-task focus cue.

Instead of 47 thoughts in 12 seconds, the brain chooses one anchor: "Follow the voice as it moves." That anchors attention. And when attention anchors, task paralysis releases, even if only for a moment.

Here's the secret: it's not the music itself. It's predictable novelty. The sound keeps changing, but in a slow, expected pattern. That blend, novelty + consistency, is the rare combination that ADHD brains thrive on. Too much novelty and you get distracted. Too much consistency and you get bored. 8D audio lives in the sweet spot.

It also works on another psychological level called attentional gating. When your brain receives rhythmic, shifting sensory input, it has less space to spin internal noise. You've basically outsourced the "where should my focus go?" decision to the sound itself. Internal decision friction disappears. No thinking required. Just follow the orbit.

And here's the part that really matters for ADHD productivity: 8D gives you a starting line.

Task paralysis is 90% failure to start. The music creates a "start ritual" that doesn't feel effortful. You don't say "focus now." You press play, and the brain automatically enters a regulated state. It's sneaky, but effective. While the sound moves, you open the laptop. You find the file. You type one line. And then you're in.

Is it clinical treatment? No. But is it a neurologically sensible, low-friction, dopamine-friendly ignition system?

Absolutely. And for a mind wired like ours, that might be enough.

Micro-activation is the whole game.

Here's the lawyer version of what works:

- Name the file.
- Insert the caption.
- Write one crappy sentence.

Not the good sentence.

Not the clever sentence.

Not the Gerry Spence sentence.

Just something.

"Comes now the Defendant…"

Boom. You're in motion.

You can fix bad paragraphs.

You cannot fix a blank page.

ADHD respects momentum, not intention.

When I'm getting ready for trial, there is one thing that absolutely has to be finished before jury selection: the trial book. And here's something most people don't understand, the trial book isn't magic. It's not some cinematic binder full of secret truths. It's just organization under pressure.

I typically have two discovery files. One stack of discovery holds everything the State ever dumped on me treated to the case. The other stack is what I believe they're actually going to use to try to put my client in a cage.

Both stacks matter, but the trial book?

That is the attack plan. It's my personal index of the case, the weak points, the contradictions, the lies I intend to expose. Without it, I walk into that courtroom blind to my own strategy. With it, I know where to spend my energy. What to hammer. What to ignore. What facts become weapons and which ones are noise.

The problem is getting started.

There have been trials where I finished the trial book the day before voir dire. There have been others where I stared at that blank binder like it was staring back at me. And my confidence? It's directly tied to whether that book is done. If it isn't, I feel like I'm walking into a heavyweight fight with one glove and a headache.

There was one relatively minor case that brought this home in the worst way. Not a murder. Not a rape. Nothing that would make the evening news. But it mattered to the man sitting next to me at counsel table. It mattered because it was his life. And like every other case, I needed to build the damn trial book.

I sat down to do it. I really did. I had all the discovery spread out like maps of a foreign country. Tabs, highlighters, paper clips — every tool of the trade within reach.

And my brain just said no.

I remember thinking: "Okay, step one… just pick the first document."

But instead: Should I reorganize this drawer?

Did I ever replace the batteries in the garage clicker?

What did that YouTube video say about polishing shoes with a dryer sheet? (I swear I looked that up.)

This is where dopamine hijacks logic. The ADHD brain doesn't respond to importance. It responds to interest. And interest is just dopamine in a trench coat pretending to be urgency. If something lights up the reward pathway, it wins. The law doesn't matter. Deadlines don't matter. The jury coming in Monday doesn't matter. Only the spark matters.

I researched anything and everything, shining shoes, vintage watches, some nonsense about replumbing a bathroom, anything except starting that trial book. It wasn't laziness; it was paralysis wearing a smile.

Inside my head, the internal monologue was a mix of shame and bargaining:

"You should be doing this."

"Just start the table of contents."

"You're screwing this up."

"Maybe ten more minutes on this other thing…"

"You're a fraud. Real lawyers don't do this."

I kept promising myself: Twenty more minutes and I'll start. My timer was going. Then another twenty. Then another. It was two full days of dancing around the task without ever crossing the activation barrier.

And here's the part that still surprises me: we hung the jury. Twelve strangers locked in a fluorescent room couldn't agree on guilt or innocence. The State didn't win, and my client didn't lose.

But the result didn't erase the truth: I almost walked into that trial unarmed, not because I didn't know what to do, but because I couldn't get myself to do it. Task paralysis isn't dramatic.

It's quiet. It's invisible. It's a thousand tiny decisions your brain refuses to make.

The jury doesn't see it. The judge doesn't see it. The client doesn't see it.

But every ADHD lawyer knows the feeling of fighting a war inside your own head while everyone else assumes you're just "not starting yet."

Start ugly, start tiny, start wrong. Just start.

The ADHD brain doesn't need inspiration. It needs ignition. Lowering the activation barrier means designing your work life around how dopamine actually behaves, not how productivity gurus pretend it behaves.

In those circumstances, the brain needs urgency. If the urgency wasn't there, the task wasn't ripe for the work to get done.

It means treating task paralysis (or any paralysis that ADHD brings to the table) as a neurological starting problem, not a character flaw. And it means understanding something I wish someone had told me twenty years ago:

The work doesn't begin when you want to start. The work begins when you make starting *impossible to avoid.*

Part III

The Cost the System Refuses to See

Chapter 12
Failure to Connect
The Blindfold the System Wears

When people talk about ADHD in the legal profession, they usually talk about it as if the problem lives entirely inside the individual lawyer. The advice always points inward. Manage your symptoms. Get organized. Improve your systems. Respect deadlines. Take your medication. Hold yourself to the standard. Every recommendation assumes that discipline is the primary variable, and that failure means the discipline was insufficient.

I believed that for a long time. I believed that if I could impose enough structure on myself—enough routine, enough self-awareness—the rest of the picture would fall into place. I treated my own wiring as the sole battleground. When something slipped, I assumed I had lost focus, failed to execute, or let myself drift.

That explanation is comforting because it keeps the problem contained. It allows the profession to say that the system works fine and that outcomes rise or fall based on personal effort alone. It also happens to be incomplete.

The Space Where the Work Actually Happens

What it leaves out is the space where the work actually happens.

Lawyers do not operate in a vacuum. We work in offices, courtrooms, chambers, conference rooms, and shared spaces that are treated as neutral by default. They are assumed to be merely background—fixed, unquestionable, and irrelevant to performance. You are expected to adapt to them without comment, regardless of how they interact with your nervous system.

For some brains, that assumption holds.

For others, it does not.

I used to walk into certain offices and feel my body tighten before I even sat down. The lighting was harsh or flickering. The hum of overhead fixtures vibrated just enough to keep my attention from settling. Printers, voices, phones, HVAC systems, and hallway traffic all competed for space in my head. Desks were arranged in open layouts that allowed every movement to register in my peripheral vision. Files were stacked everywhere—not because anyone was careless, but because volume demanded it.

None of this was considered remarkable.

It was called a workplace.

For me, it was cognitive friction layered on top of cognitive friction. Every sensory input demanded processing. Every interruption pulled attention sideways. The space itself became something I had to work against before I could even begin the work.

That is where the profession's blind spot begins.

When the Room Never Recedes

The legal system treats space as neutral because it assumes a brain that can filter, dampen, and ignore what is not immediately relevant. If you have that kind of brain, the room fades into the background and the work comes forward. If you do not, the room never recedes. It stays present—loud, demanding, and insistent—even when you are trying to think.

Performance does not come from discipline alone. It comes from the interaction between mind and environment. When those two are mismatched, effort does not translate cleanly into output. The quality of the work begins to reflect the conditions under which it is produced rather than the intelligence or commitment of the person doing it.

I learned this long before I had language for it.

I remember sitting in a converted office space with no windows and fluorescent panels that pulsed just enough to disrupt my concentration. The desk was cluttered with files that were not mine. Every surface carried someone else's unfinished business. I tried to work through it the way I had been taught— by forcing myself forward and ignoring the discomfort.

Nothing stuck.

Each time I began a task, something in the room pulled my attention away. A flicker. A sound. A movement I could not screen out. I felt alert and exhausted at the same time, as if my nervous system was on constant watch. At one point, I found myself staring at a blank document, unable to make my fingers move. I remember thinking that this must be a personal failing. Other people worked in environments like this every day. Other lawyers handled heavier loads under worse conditions. If I could not focus here, maybe I simply was not built for this work.

That is what an unfriendly environment does when the profession refuses to name it.

It turns a structural problem into a private indictment.

The truth was simpler and harder to accept. The room itself was undermining my ability to function.

From Structure to Indictment

There is research now showing what many people with ADHD have lived without explanation. Light intensity and color temperature affect alertness, working memory, and emotional regulation. Flicker and glare increase cognitive load. Unpredictable sensory input taxes executive function. Disrupted sleep compounds all of it. None of this is controversial science. It is well documented.

Yet when lawyers are evaluated by disciplinary bodies, environment rarely appears anywhere in the analysis. Missed deadlines, delayed communication, disorganization, and inconsistency are treated as moral signals rather than functional symptoms. The system measures outcomes and assigns character explanations to them. It does not ask whether the conditions under which the work was done made those outcomes more likely.

The disciplinary process reads as if executive function exists in isolation. It focuses on what happened, not why it happened.

It assumes that if a lawyer struggled to initiate tasks, keep time, or manage administrative demands, the cause must be indifference or neglect. The possibility that those struggles reflect a recognized disability interacting with a hostile environment is rarely explored.

That omission is not accidental.

It keeps the narrative clean.

Why the System Prefers the Blindfold

The legal profession does not misunderstand ADHD by accident. It misunderstands it because misunderstanding is efficient.

Systems are built to process volume. They rely on categorization, standardization, and repeatable judgments. When something goes wrong, the system asks questions that can be answered quickly: Was the deadline met. Was the filing complete. Was the response timely. Those questions produce clean answers. Yes or no. On time or late. Compliant or deficient.

Context complicates that process.

Once you ask why something happened, the analysis slows down. You have to examine conditions, capacity, competing demands, and environmental factors. You have to acknowledge that two lawyers may perform the same task under very different cognitive loads. You have to confront the possibility that the system itself contributed to the outcome it is now judging.

That kind of inquiry is expensive. It takes time. It requires nuance. It introduces uncertainty into processes that are designed to eliminate it.

Moral explanations are cheaper.

If a missed deadline can be labeled carelessness, the analysis ends. If a delayed response can be labeled indifference, no further inquiry is required. If inconsistency can be framed as unreliability, the system does not have to ask whether the structure it imposed was reasonable or accessible. The blame stays contained within the individual, and the machinery keeps moving.

This is not malice. It is incentive.

Administrative Ease Over Functional Truth

Disciplinary systems, administrative bodies, and courts are under constant pressure to resolve matters efficiently. They are rewarded for closure, not comprehension. A narrative that locates failure inside a person is easier to administer than one that requires examining the interaction between person and environment. It preserves the appearance of objectivity while avoiding uncomfortable questions about design.

Disability disrupts that simplicity.

Once ADHD is treated as a functional impairment rather than a character flaw, the system is forced to slow down. It has to ask whether expectations were calibrated to reality. It has to consider whether accommodation was possible. It has to distinguish between unwillingness and inability. Those distinctions do not fit neatly into checklists or timelines.

So the system resists them.

It is easier to pretend that all lawyers start with the same cognitive equipment and operate under neutral conditions. It is easier to treat variation as deviation rather than difference. It is easier to punish outcomes than to examine inputs.

The blindfold serves a purpose. It allows the profession to benefit from the strengths of lawyers with ADHD—intensity, responsiveness, creativity, adaptability—without accounting for the cost of extracting those strengths under hostile conditions. When performance falters, the system can point to the falter as proof that the individual was the problem all along.

That narrative protects the structure. It protects the process. And it does so at the expense of understanding.

Once you see that incentive clearly, the pattern stops looking accidental. The blindfold is not ignorance. It is a choice to prioritize administrative ease over functional truth. And as long as that choice remains unexamined, the same misunderstandings will continue to repeat, no matter how many individual lawyers are disciplined along the way.

When Context is Explicitly Excluded

I came face to face with that reality when my own work was examined without any interest in context. The questions were framed to fit a checklist. Why did this slip. Why did that take longer. Why was this not completed sooner. The room where the work occurred was treated as irrelevant. Lighting, noise, sensory load, volume, and structure did not factor into the analysis. Only the behavior mattered.

The environment was part of the story.

It was simply not a story the system wanted to hear.

Disability Law Versus Professional Discipline

This is where the gap between disability law and professional discipline becomes impossible to ignore. ADHD is a disability under federal law. Executive function is a major life activity. The ability to plan, organize, initiate tasks, manage time, and sustain attention is central to legal practice. When those functions are impaired, the impairment is neurological—not moral.

The ADA does not eliminate responsibility. It reshapes how responsibility is understood. It requires inquiry into whether conduct is linked to disability. It requires consideration of reasonable accommodation before punishment. It recognizes that a person may be fully capable of performing essential functions if the conditions under which those functions are carried out do not actively interfere with them.

The legal profession often resists that framework when it applies to its own members. Once impairment is acknowledged, the system would have to confront uncomfortable questions. Are our workspaces functional. Are our expectations calibrated to real cognitive limits. Are we evaluating competence, or merely compliance with structures that were never designed for everyone.

Avoiding those questions preserves the illusion that the system itself is neutral.

The Cost of Maintaining the Illusion

I have watched what happens when that illusion is maintained. Lawyers internalize blame for symptoms they did not choose. They work longer hours to compensate. They build habits that keep them afloat temporarily but erode sustainability. They mask until they cannot. When the mask cracks, the system points to the crack as proof that something was always wrong.

The cost is not just professional.

It is personal.

There were periods in my career when I knew I was capable of high-level advocacy in the courtroom while simultaneously struggling with the administrative machinery that surrounded it. That contradiction made no sense to me at first. How could someone be sharp, prepared, and effective under pressure, yet inconsistent behind the scenes?

The answer was not effort.

It was context.

The cognitive demands of a courtroom are structured and immediate. The demands of an office are diffuse and abstract. One environment supplies urgency and clarity. The other requires internal regulation an ADHD brain does not reliably generate on its own. When the environment amplifies strengths, performance looks elite. When it amplifies weaknesses, performance looks deficient.

The profession tends to notice only the result.

How Discipline Actually Gets Triggered

Consider how professional discipline is typically triggered.

A deadline is missed. A filing is late. A communication is delayed. The initiating fact is binary: the thing was done on time or it was not. Once that fact is established, the inquiry begins from a presumption that the failure reflects a choice.

Why did you not file on time.

Why did you wait until the last moment.

Why did you fail to respond sooner.

Each question assumes that the lawyer experienced time, urgency, and initiation the same way the system does. Each assumes that the lawyer had full access to executive function at the relevant moment. Each assumes that the only meaningful variable is effort.

What the questions do not ask is equally important.

They do not ask where the work was done.

They do not ask how many competing demands were active at the time.

They do not ask whether the lawyer's disability affects time perception, initiation, or working memory.

They do not ask whether the structure of the task itself made timely completion predictably difficult for someone with ADHD.

Those questions are excluded not because they are irrelevant, but because the procedure is not designed to hear them.

Once the inquiry is framed around conduct alone, explanation becomes indistinguishable from excuse. Any attempt to describe cognitive load, environmental interference, or executive function impairment sounds like avoidance, even when it is accurate. The process rewards answers that accept fault quickly and punishes answers that introduce context.

By the time the decision is made, the outcome feels orderly. The rule was clear. The deadline was known. The behavior deviated. Discipline follows.

What disappears in that sequence is the possibility that the system itself contributed to the failure. The structure of the inquiry never allowed that question to be asked.

Where Law Falls Behind

Other fields have begun to grapple with this distinction. Medicine, education, and federal employment systems increasingly separate misconduct from impairment. They ask whether accommodation would address the issue. They recognize that supporting function can be more protective than punishment.

Law lags behind, in part because it clings to a mythology of uniform competence. The belief that a good lawyer should function anywhere, under any conditions, without accommodation is deeply ingrained. It is also unrealistic.

The environments in which we work matter. They shape attention, energy, and execution. Ignoring that fact does not make the profession rigorous. It makes it careless.

Seeing the Structure Clearly

The blindfold the system wears is not ignorance. It is a choice to simplify. It allows the profession to treat outcomes as isolated data points instead of signals produced by an interaction between person and structure. It allows discipline to proceed without asking whether design contributed to failure.

Once you see that, the landscape shifts. The question is no longer whether an individual lawyer tried hard enough. The question becomes whether the system created conditions under which effort could succeed.

That recognition does not excuse mistakes.

It contextualizes them.

It opens the door to solutions that actually work.

If the profession is serious about competence, it has to be serious about environment. If it is serious about accountability, it has to be willing to examine its own structures. And if it claims to respect the law, it cannot continue to ignore disability principles when they apply to its own ranks.

The blindfold is optional. Removing it requires honesty about how lawyers actually work, where they struggle, and why. Until that happens, too many careers will be judged without ever being understood.

That is not justice.

It is convenience.

And convenience has always been easier than seeing what is right in front of you.

Chapter 13
Invisible Labor, Invisible Debt
Emotional Load and Cognitive Spillover

There is work happening in the background of many legal careers that never appears on a timesheet, never shows up in a disciplinary record, and never earns credit when things go right. It is not legal analysis. It is not advocacy. It is not preparation in the traditional sense. It is regulation.

This is the constant, low-level labor of managing reactions, smoothing tension, anticipating disappointment, recalibrating tone, deciding when to speak and when to stay quiet, deciding how much of yourself to reveal and how much to conceal. It is the work of staying acceptable in rooms that are not built for the way your mind processes pressure.

For lawyers with ADHD, this labor is not occasional. It is continuous. It runs underneath every client interaction, every courtroom appearance, every email drafted and redrafted to avoid sounding abrupt, careless, or difficult. It is the effort of appearing steady when steadiness does not come for free.

The problem is not that this labor exists. The problem is that it is invisible.

Because it is invisible, it is treated as weightless. Because it is treated as weightless, it is never factored into assessments of capacity. And because it is never factored in, lawyers are routinely evaluated as though they are operating with the same reserves as everyone else.

They are not.

Over time, that mismatch creates debt. Not emotional debt in the abstract sense, but cognitive debt. Energy spent regulating cannot be spent analyzing. Attention spent monitoring reactions cannot be spent planning. Margin absorbed by social friction is margin no longer available when something actually goes wrong.

The lawyer keeps working. The system keeps expecting. The account keeps draining.

This chapter is about naming that drain. Not as a complaint, and not as an excuse, but as a structural reality the profession consistently fails to see. Until that reality is acknowledged, performance will continue to be measured without context, and collapse will continue to arrive as a surprise.

There is a form of exhaustion that never shows up on a time sheet.

It does not announce itself as stress or burnout. It does not arrive with a dramatic failure or a missed deadline. Most of the time, it is invisible. The work still gets done. Court appearances still happen. Clients are still represented competently. From the outside, nothing appears wrong.

Inside, something is leaking.

The legal profession treats emotion as noise. Something to be managed, suppressed, or ignored in favor of logic and discipline. Lawyers are trained early to separate feeling from function, to compartmentalize, to maintain composure regardless of circumstance. That expectation is not inherently unreasonable. The problem is that it assumes emotion behaves the same way in every nervous system.

It does not.

For lawyers with ADHD, emotional input does not stay contained. It spreads. It occupies working memory. It competes with planning, initiation, and prioritization. It does not disappear simply because the task in front of you is technical or routine. The brain keeps processing it in the background, quietly consuming bandwidth that the profession assumes is available for work.

This is not about being emotional. It is about carrying load.

Every difficult client interaction adds weight. Every unresolved conflict with opposing counsel takes up space. Every moment of judicial tension, every ambiguous ruling, every unanswered email that might matter later—all of it occupies cognitive real estate. Most lawyers experience this as background pressure. Lawyers with ADHD experience it as signal.

That distinction matters.

The ADHD brain does not filter emotional input efficiently. It does not triage relevance the way the profession expects. Emotional information arrives with urgency, regardless of whether it deserves it. A frustrated client call does not end when the call ends. A tense hearing does not stop reverberating when court adjourns. The nervous system keeps processing long after the event has passed.

This is how capacity erodes without warning.

From the outside, it looks like the lawyer is still functioning. From the inside, the margin is gone. Tasks that once felt manageable begin to require more effort. Initiation slows. Time perception warps. The calendar feels heavier than it should. Nothing has changed on paper. Everything has changed in practice.

The profession has no language for this.

Lawyers are evaluated based on output. Deadlines met. Filings completed. Responses timely. There is no column for cognitive load. No accounting for emotional spillover. No recognition that a lawyer who spent the morning absorbing other people's fear, anger, or disappointment is not starting the afternoon with the same resources as someone who did not.

For a brain already managing time blindness, initiation friction, and executive function strain, this uncounted load matters. It explains why some days feel inexplicably harder than others. It explains why the same task can feel effortless one week and impossible the next. It explains why a lawyer can be fully capable, fully committed, and still find themselves stalled in ways that make no sense on paper.

This is not fragility. It is math.

Working memory is finite. Attention is finite. Emotional processing draws from the same pool the profession assumes is reserved for work. When that pool is depleted, performance degrades—not catastrophically, not immediately, but subtly. A missed call here. A delayed response there. A growing sense of pressure without a clear source.

By the time the degradation becomes visible, the narrative is already forming.

The system sees behavior. It does not see load.

A lawyer who misses a deadline is labeled disorganized. A lawyer who delays a response is labeled inattentive. A lawyer who struggles to initiate work is labeled unmotivated. The system does not ask what else that lawyer was carrying. It does not ask whether the cognitive cost of the work environment itself has exceeded the brain's ability to compensate.

This is especially dangerous in adversarial practice.

Criminal defense, litigation, and trial work place lawyers in constant contact with high-stakes emotion. Fear, anger, grief, desperation, hostility—these are not occasional features of the job. They are the material. The profession assumes lawyers can absorb that material without consequence. For many, that assumption holds. For lawyers with ADHD, it does not.

Emotion does not stay in its lane.

It bleeds into time perception. It distorts urgency. It interferes with initiation. It amplifies task paralysis. It makes future planning feel heavier than it should. None of this is visible to the system until something slips. By then, the explanation sounds like excuse rather than mechanism.

That is the trap.

Lawyers with ADHD often blame themselves for this erosion. They assume the problem is discipline, resilience, or professionalism. They push harder. They work longer. They ignore the accumulating load because the profession has taught them that noticing it is weakness.

It is not. It is awareness of a variable the system refuses to measure.

This chapter exists to name that variable. Not to pathologize emotion. Not to excuse mistakes. Not to argue that law should be easier. It exists to explain why performance cannot be evaluated accurately without understanding what the brain is carrying beneath the surface.

Until emotional load is acknowledged as a real, measurable drain on cognitive capacity, the profession will continue to misread behavior. Lawyers will continue to be judged for outcomes that make sense only when stripped of context. And people with ADHD will continue to wonder why competence feels so fragile in a career they are otherwise built to do well.

What follows is not theory. It is anatomy.

It is an explanation of how emotional input becomes cognitive spillover, why that spillover matters more in ADHD, and how ignoring it distorts everything the system thinks it understands about performance, reliability, and responsibility.

Once you see it, the pattern becomes impossible to unsee.

There are days when I would walk out of court feeling steady. The hearing goes as expected. I do the work. The judge listens. Nothing dramatic happens, which is usually the point. From the hallway, it looks like momentum.

By the time I sit down at my desk back at the office, that momentum is gone. The urgency that carried me through court drains away, and the work in front of me suddenly feels heavier than it should. I open emails, pull up files, reread things I already understand. Everything is familiar. Nothing starts.

I tell myself to begin small. One email. One paragraph. One sentence. I draft, delete, adjust, and save without sending. I move between tasks without finishing any of them. Time passes, but there is nothing concrete to show for it. From the outside, it would look like procrastination. Inside, it feels like depletion.

Court demanded constant regulation: attention, restraint, timing, tone. I paid that cost without noticing it while I was there. The office offers no structure to replace it. No urgency. No external pressure. Just work that assumes the same version of me still exists.

That gap between performance and aftermath is rarely acknowledged. Court counts. Results count. What it costs to get there does not. The energy spent regulating attention, emotion, and timing disappears the moment the hearing ends. When the lawyer returns to the office depleted and struggles to initiate the next task, the system reads that as delay, not depletion. Over time, that uncounted effort accumulates. Not as failure, but as invisible labor—and the debt it creates is what this chapter is really about. That residue has a name.

Cognitive Carryover Debt is the residue the profession refuses to acknowledge.

It is the cognitive cost of staying regulated, credible, and effective under pressure, carried forward into the rest of the day.

Nothing resets just because the calendar says it should.

You leave court having spent judgment, restraint, anticipation, emotional regulation, and strategic focus. The argument may be over and the ruling entered, but the load does not stay behind. It follows you back to the office and quietly draws down capacity you were expected to still have.

This is the labor that never appears on a timesheet but always shows up in outcomes. By the time the system notices it, the debt has already compounded.

How Emotional Load Consumes Working Memory

Working memory is the workspace of the brain. It is where information is held temporarily so it can be used, manipulated, prioritized, and acted upon. Every lawyer relies on it constantly. It is what allows you to keep a hearing schedule in mind while drafting a motion, to remember what a client said while responding to a judge's question, to track strategy while listening to testimony.

It is also limited.

The profession tends to treat working memory as stable and renewable, something that resets between tasks. That assumption holds reasonably well for many people. It does not hold for everyone. For lawyers with ADHD, working memory is more vulnerable to intrusion, and emotional input is one of the most potent intruders.

Emotional information does not wait its turn.

A difficult client call does not simply register as a discrete event and then clear. It continues processing in the background.

The brain replays it, evaluates it, anticipates consequences, imagines future conversations. That activity draws from the same pool of resources used to plan, initiate, and execute legal work. Nothing about that drain is visible, but it is real.

This is where the mismatch between expectation and reality begins.

A lawyer may sit down to draft a motion with full intention to work. The law is familiar. The structure is clear. On paper, the task should be straightforward. Yet the mind feels crowded. Focus slips. Initiation stalls. The problem is not complexity. The problem is that the workspace is already occupied.

Emotional load consumes slots.

Every unresolved interpersonal interaction occupies a position in working memory. Every ambiguous ruling that might matter later. Every email that could escalate. Every concern about how a judge interpreted something you said. None of these items are frivolous. In law, they often matter. The issue is that they do not release their grip simply because you have moved on to a different task.

For an ADHD brain, release does not come easily.

The filtering mechanisms that allow other people to defer emotional processing are less efficient. The brain does not reliably say, "This can wait." It keeps the information active, even when it is not immediately useful. That persistence creates crowding. The more crowded the workspace becomes, the harder it is to bring new tasks online.

This is why emotional days feel different from purely technical ones.

A morning spent in court, absorbing tension, uncertainty, and adversarial energy, leaves less capacity for afternoon administrative work. Not because the lawyer is tired in a conventional sense, but because the brain is still processing. The system assumes the lawyer should be able to pivot seamlessly. The brain disagrees.

The cost shows up as friction.

Tasks take longer to start. Simple decisions feel heavier. Time perception blurs. Initiation feels effortful in ways that do not match the task itself. The lawyer may interpret this as laziness or lack of discipline. The system may interpret it the same way. Neither interpretation is accurate.

What is happening is saturation.

When working memory is saturated, the brain prioritizes survival over efficiency. It becomes reactive rather than deliberate. It attends to whatever feels most emotionally charged, not what is most strategically important. That is not a choice. It is a shift in operating mode.

This is particularly dangerous in law, where so much work depends on sustained, low-stimulation tasks. Drafting, reviewing, organizing, responding—these activities require available cognitive space. They do not generate their own urgency. They rely on the brain's ability to hold future consequences in mind while acting in the present.

When emotional load occupies that space, those tasks suffer first.

The profession tends to misread this sequence. It assumes the lawyer is prioritizing poorly. In reality, the lawyer is operating with reduced capacity. The distinction matters, because the solution is different. You cannot discipline your way out of saturation. You have to reduce load or change how work is structured around it.

This is also why performance can appear inconsistent.

A lawyer may perform exceptionally well in court, where emotional intensity is immediate and structured, and then struggle afterward with tasks that appear objectively easier. The system reads this as contradiction. In truth, it is continuity. Court consumes capacity. The bill comes due later.

For lawyers with ADHD, this pattern is amplified.

Emotional input is louder. It persists longer. It competes more aggressively for attention. Without intentional boundaries, the cognitive spillover accumulates until it begins to distort performance in ways that feel inexplicable to everyone involved.

Including the lawyer.

This is not a character flaw. It is not oversensitivity. It is not lack of professionalism. It is a predictable interaction between emotional labor and executive function in a brain that does not filter efficiently.

Until that interaction is acknowledged, lawyers will continue to blame themselves for failures that originate upstream. Systems will continue to evaluate behavior without accounting for load. And the gap between expectation and reality will keep widening.

The next section addresses what the profession does with this blind spot—and why misreading emotional spillover as behavioral failure leads to outcomes that feel orderly on paper and unjust in practice.

How Emotional Labor Becomes Invisible Debt

One of the most dangerous misunderstandings in the legal profession is the belief that work only counts when it leaves a visible trail. Filings count. Court appearances count. Emails count. Billing entries count. What happens inside a lawyer's head rarely does.

That assumption breaks down badly for lawyers with ADHD, because a disproportionate amount of their effort is spent managing emotional load long before anything observable ever happens.

Emotional labor is not an add-on to the work. It is not a soft skill layered on top of legal analysis. For many lawyers, especially those with ADHD, emotional regulation is a prerequisite for doing the work at all. Before a single document is drafted, the nervous system has already been negotiating urgency, filtering threat, suppressing distraction, tracking tone, anticipating reactions, and managing the internal cost of conflict. That labor does not show up on a docket. It does not produce a timestamp. It does not create a paper trail. But it consumes capacity.

A lawyer with ADHD often begins the day already partially depleted, not because they are disorganized or unfocused, but because their brain has been running background processes since the moment they woke up. Who needs to be called back. Which conversation is going to be difficult. Which case feels emotionally charged. Which deadline is approaching but still feels unreal. Which client is anxious. Which judge is unpredictable. Each of these elements demands attention before the "real work" even begins.

From the outside, none of this is visible. From the inside, it is constant.

The profession tends to treat emotional labor as either irrelevant or infinite. If you are good with people, if clients trust you, if judges respond to you, if juries listen, those traits are praised without acknowledgment of their cost. The expectation is that you will simply continue to absorb the emotional weight of the work indefinitely, without erosion.

That expectation is wrong.

Emotional labor behaves like debt. It does not cause immediate failure. It allows the system to keep functioning—often impressively—right up until the point it can no longer be carried. And when it finally comes due, the consequences appear suddenly, without context.

This is why so many lawyers with ADHD appear to be doing well until they are not.

They are not coasting. They are carrying.

They are carrying the emotional volatility of clients whose lives are unraveling. They are carrying the anticipatory stress of hearings that have not yet arrived. They are carrying the unspoken pressure of needing to perform competence in rooms that are hostile to their nervous system. They are carrying unresolved tasks that have not yet triggered urgency but still occupy mental space. They are carrying conversations that have not happened yet but already feel exhausting.

All of that takes energy. All of that consumes executive function. And none of it registers as "work" in the system's accounting.

The problem is not that this debt exists. The problem is that it accumulates silently.

Because emotional labor does not announce itself, there is no external signal that capacity is being drained. There is no warning light on the dashboard. From the outside, everything looks normal. The lawyer is still showing up. Still arguing well. Still producing outcomes. Still responding, mostly, on time.

The system interprets this as stability.

But stability built on invisible depletion is fragile.

When the bill finally arrives, it does not arrive labeled as emotional exhaustion or cognitive overload. It arrives as missed deadlines. Delayed responses. Dropped balls. Inconsistent follow-through. Administrative slippage. The system sees only the outcome, not the accumulation that made it inevitable.

This is where narratives form quickly and unfairly.

The lawyer "used to be reliable." The lawyer "is slipping." The lawyer "can't manage their practice." The lawyer "lost focus." The lawyer "stopped caring."

None of those narratives account for the fact that the lawyer has been paying interest on invisible debt for years.

What makes this especially dangerous for lawyers with ADHD is the timing. Emotional labor does not degrade performance gradually. It degrades margin. Things still get done, but with less room for error. Less buffer. Less recovery time. Less flexibility when something unexpected happens.

Eventually, several things come due at once.

A client escalates emotionally. A judge compresses a timeline. A filing deadline collides with a hearing. An administrative task that has been deferred because it never felt urgent suddenly becomes critical. The emotional load spikes at the exact moment executive function is already compromised.

That is when failure becomes visible.

From the inside, it feels abrupt and bewildering. From the outside, it looks like negligence emerging without warning. The system responds to what it can see, and what it can see is the missed step—not the years of unseen labor that preceded it.

This is why lawyers with ADHD often struggle to explain what went wrong in ways the system will accept. They are trying to describe depletion, saturation, and delayed consequence in a language built for discrete acts and timestamps. The system asks, "Why didn't you do this?" when the real question is, "What did it cost you to keep doing everything else?"

That question is rarely asked.

The failure to recognize emotional labor as real work creates a structural blind spot. It allows the profession to benefit from the strengths of ADHD lawyers—empathy, intensity, responsiveness, adaptability—while refusing to account for the toll those strengths take over time. The work is celebrated. The cost is ignored. When the cost finally surfaces, it is treated as a personal lapse rather than an accumulated debt.

This is not a character problem. It is an accounting problem.

Until the system learns to see emotional labor as part of the workload, it will continue to misinterpret the moment when that labor finally overwhelms capacity. Lawyers will continue to be judged for outcomes without acknowledgment of inputs. And people with ADHD will continue to carry weight that no one else seems to notice—until it drops.

Chapter 14
Systemic Misreading
Why ADHD Behavior is Interpreted as Defiance

Most professional systems are not designed to understand how work actually happens. They are designed to record outcomes. What gets filed on time. What gets returned promptly. What appears consistent on paper. Everything else is background noise.

This works well enough when performance follows predictable patterns. It breaks down when it does not.

The legal profession, in particular, relies heavily on proxies. Responsiveness stands in for engagement. Organization stands in for diligence. Consistency stands in for competence. These shortcuts are not malicious. They are practical. Courts are busy. Firms are busy. Regulators are busy. No system can fully examine intent, context, environment, or cognitive load every time it evaluates a lawyer's conduct. Instead, it looks at what it can see.

The problem is that what can be seen is often incomplete.

For a lawyer with ADHD, performance is rarely uniform across settings. Work that involves urgency, human interaction, and live decision-making often looks strong, sometimes exceptional. Work that involves delayed consequences, quiet follow-through, or abstract time horizons can look uneven. The system is not built to reconcile those two truths. It tends to assume that one of them must be the real version of the lawyer and the other an aberration.

That assumption drives misinterpretation.

When a lawyer is articulate in court but slow to respond to email, the system often reads the delay as indifference. When filings are thoughtful but occasionally late, the system reads that as poor prioritization. When preparation is deep but administrative tasks lag, the system reads that as disorganization. None of those readings account for how executive function actually works in a brain that processes urgency and time differently.

The system does not ask whether the lawyer is working hard. It asks whether the work appears on schedule. It does not ask whether the lawyer understands their obligations. It asks whether those obligations are reflected in the record. This is not cruelty. It is design.

The misreading happens when behavior is evaluated without its operating context.

Consider how many professional judgments are made based on silence. A call not returned quickly enough. An email answered later than expected. A task completed close to the deadline rather than comfortably ahead of it. Silence is easy to interpret. It invites inference. The inference usually chosen is the simplest one. The lawyer did not care enough. The lawyer was not paying attention. The lawyer let something slide.

What rarely enters the analysis is whether the lawyer was managing competing demands that did not announce themselves equally. Whether the task that appears delayed was competing with a task that felt urgent in a neurological sense. Whether the lawyer's attention was being pulled by immediate human consequences rather than distant procedural ones. Whether the environment they were working in made initiation slower or tracking harder.

The system is not curious about those questions. It assumes they are irrelevant.

This is where misunderstanding takes root. The legal profession tends to treat consistency as a moral attribute rather than a neurological one. If a lawyer can perform well sometimes, the logic goes, then they should be able to perform well all the time. Variability is read as choice. When variability appears, intent is inferred.

That inference is often wrong.

How the System Decides What Behavior Means

The legal system does not begin by asking how a lawyer's brain works. It begins by asking what happened.

That distinction matters.

Law is built on observable conduct. Filings are late or timely. Responses are made or missed. Appearances happen or they do not. From those facts, the system draws conclusions about reliability, diligence, judgment, and professionalism. This approach works reasonably well when behavior is a reliable proxy for capacity. With ADHD, it is not.

The system assumes a linear chain: ability → effort → behavior → outcome.

When the outcome is defective, the inference runs backward. The lawyer must have failed to manage time, failed to prioritize, failed to care enough.

That inference feels neutral. It feels objective. It is neither.

ADHD disrupts the connection between intention and execution. Not occasionally, but structurally. Initiation, time perception, emotional regulation, and working memory fluctuate based on context, load, and urgency. As a result, behavior no longer maps cleanly onto effort or competence.

The system does not see that disruption. It sees only the surface.

This is why two identical behaviors can mean radically different things depending on the brain producing them. A delayed response may reflect neglect in one lawyer and cognitive saturation in another. A missed step may signal disorganization or an executive function bottleneck. The legal system treats those possibilities as interchangeable because it does not recognize mechanism as relevant.

Once behavior is detached from mechanism, misreading becomes inevitable.

The system believes it is evaluating professionalism. In reality, it is evaluating compliance with structures that assume a neurotypical relationship to time, attention, and initiation. When a lawyer with ADHD fails to meet those expectations, the failure is interpreted as character rather than constraint.

This is not malice. It is compression.

The system compresses complex cognitive processes into simple narratives because those narratives are administratively efficient. They allow decisions to be made quickly, responsibility to be assigned cleanly, and discipline to proceed without ambiguity.

What they do not allow is accuracy.

That is the core problem this chapter addresses. Not that lawyers with ADHD make mistakes, but that the meaning assigned to those mistakes is often wrong. And once the meaning is wrong, every response that follows is miscalibrated.

ADHD does not impair intelligence, ethics, or commitment. It alters how attention is activated, how time is perceived, and how tasks are initiated. Those differences do not announce themselves. They leave traces. Delays. Gaps. Uneven pacing. The system sees the traces and fills in the story.

Once a story forms, it is remarkably durable.

Professional systems have a tendency to backfill explanations. If a lawyer is labeled disorganized, future behavior is filtered through that label. Neutral events begin to look confirmatory. A late filing becomes part of a pattern. A slow response reinforces an impression. The original cause of the behavior becomes less important than the coherence of the narrative.

This process does not require bad faith. It only requires incomplete information and a preference for clean explanations.

The danger here is subtle. The lawyer is not being evaluated on the quality of their thinking or the substance of their advocacy. They are being evaluated on surface indicators that are imperfect proxies for those things. When the proxies fail to map accurately onto the underlying work, the evaluation becomes distorted.

That distortion affects more than formal discipline. It affects reputation. It affects trust. It affects how much margin the lawyer is given when something does go wrong. It affects whether explanations are believed or dismissed.

Most lawyers with ADHD will never encounter a disciplinary body. Many will have long, successful careers. The misreading happens earlier and more quietly than that. It happens in performance reviews. In hallway conversations. In the unspoken assumptions that shape how others respond to them.

This is why context matters so much. When systems do not understand how a behavior arises, they tend to moralize it. What is actually a function of attention regulation becomes framed as attitude. What is a timing issue becomes framed as reliability. What is a neurological lag becomes framed as disregard.

Once framed that way, the burden shifts entirely onto the individual. Fix yourself. Do better. Be more consistent. The system does not examine whether its expectations align with how human cognition actually works. It assumes the problem is internal and individual.

That assumption is convenient. It absolves the system of responsibility. It also misses the point.

Understanding how systems misread behavior is not about avoiding accountability. It is about accuracy. Accountability without accurate diagnosis solves nothing. It creates pressure without improvement. It punishes symptoms while leaving causes untouched.

For lawyers with ADHD, the solution is not to fear evaluation. It is to understand how evaluation works. Systems will always rely on what they can see. That will not change. What can change is whether the record contains context, structure, and explanation before misinterpretation fills the gap.

The moment behavior is separated from context, the story writes itself. The goal is not to argue with the story after the fact. The goal is to prevent the wrong one from forming in the first place.

That is not alarmism. It is realism.

How Context Disappears

Context rarely vanishes all at once. It erodes.

When a system evaluates behavior, it does so by narrowing its field of vision. It reduces complexity to categories it knows how to process. Deadlines are either met or missed. Communications are either timely or delayed. Files are either organized or not. That narrowing is not malicious. It is procedural. Systems survive by simplifying what they observe.

The trouble begins when simplification becomes substitution.

In law, behavior is almost always evaluated after the fact. The file is reviewed in a quiet room, long after the noise, pressure, and competing demands that shaped the conduct have passed. The evaluator sees the end result without ever experiencing the conditions under which it occurred. What remains on the page looks clean. What produced it was not.

Context disappears because it is inconvenient. It does not fit neatly into checklists or rules. It resists standardization. And once it is gone, interpretation rushes in to fill the gap.

The legal profession is especially vulnerable to this distortion because it treats outcomes as proxies for intent. A missed deadline is read as neglect. A delayed response becomes indifference. A pattern of inconsistency is labeled unreliability. These interpretations feel reasonable because the system assumes that everyone experiences time, workload, and cognitive strain in roughly the same way.

That assumption is wrong, but it is deeply embedded.

Most systems are built around what is observable and repeatable. They reward traits that produce steady, linear output. They struggle to account for performance that fluctuates with environment, urgency, or cognitive load. When variability appears, the system looks for explanations it already understands. Personal responsibility. Professionalism. Judgment.

Context does not survive that translation.

What gets lost first is the surrounding pressure. The overlapping deadlines. The sudden emergencies. The constant interruptions. The cumulative fatigue that comes from operating without margin. None of those things leave clear fingerprints on a docket sheet or a case log. They exist in the lived experience of the person doing the work, not in the record the system later reviews.

What disappears next is internal effort. The hours spent trying to start. The repeated attempts to engage with a task that would not activate. The false starts. The mental rewrites. The work done that never became visible because it did not produce a clean output in time. Systems tend to count results, not attempts.

Finally, what disappears entirely is the environment itself. The space where the work occurred. The noise. The lighting. The interruptions. The lack of control over pace and sequence. The way attention was pulled and fractured throughout the day. The system treats the workspace as neutral because it has no mechanism for measuring its impact.

Once those layers are stripped away, the behavior stands alone.

And alone, it is easy to misread.

This is how context disappears without anyone consciously removing it. The process is incremental. Each step feels reasonable. Each omission seems minor. By the time interpretation is complete, the original conditions are no longer part of the story at all.

What remains is a narrative built from fragments.

That narrative tends to harden quickly because systems prefer stability. Once a pattern is identified, subsequent behavior is filtered through it. New facts are not evaluated fresh. They are used to confirm what the system already believes it has learned. Context rarely makes it back into the frame once this happens.

For lawyers with ADHD, this dynamic is particularly dangerous because so much of what affects performance is invisible from the outside. Executive function does not fail loudly. It fails quietly. Task initiation issues do not announce themselves. Time blindness does not look like defiance. Cognitive overload does not always produce chaos. Often, it produces delay, compression, and inconsistency.

Those outcomes are easy to see. Their causes are not.

The profession tends to assume that if someone is capable of excellent performance in one setting, they should be capable of consistent performance in all settings. When that consistency does not appear, the explanation defaults to effort or character. The possibility that the same lawyer is operating under radically different cognitive conditions from hour to hour rarely enters the analysis.

Context is not just background. It is an active force. It shapes how attention is allocated, how tasks are prioritized, and how time is perceived. When context disappears, behavior is flattened into something it never actually was.

This flattening is not neutral. It favors people whose internal systems align with institutional expectations. It disadvantages those whose performance is more sensitive to environment, timing, and structure. The system does not intend this outcome, but intention is irrelevant to impact.

Once context is gone, correction becomes difficult. The person being evaluated is often placed in the position of having to explain what cannot easily be proven. Internal experience does not translate cleanly into external evidence. Environmental strain does not show up in a time log. Cognitive load does not appear in an email chain.

The system asks for explanations using the wrong language.

It wants reasons that fit its categories. It wants assurances that behavior will change without asking what conditions made the behavior likely in the first place. It wants certainty in a domain where certainty was never available.

This is why context cannot be an afterthought. Once it disappears, it rarely returns on its own. If it is not introduced early and deliberately, the story that replaces it will harden into something else.

The failure to preserve context is not a failure of compassion. It is a failure of design. Systems are doing what they were built to do. The problem is that they were built around a narrow model of how people work.

Understanding this shifts the question. The issue is no longer whether someone should be held accountable. Accountability remains. The issue is whether accountability is being assessed against a complete picture or a truncated one.

When context disappears, accountability does not disappear with it. It simply becomes misaligned.

The goal is not to excuse behavior by pointing to context. The goal is to evaluate behavior in light of it. That distinction matters. One avoids responsibility. The other defines it accurately.

This is the point where many conversations about performance break down. People fear that acknowledging context weakens standards. In reality, it strengthens them.

Standards applied without context are blunt instruments. Standards applied with context are precise.

The legal profession prides itself on precision. It demands it from lawyers. It should demand it from itself.

If context keeps disappearing, it is not because it is irrelevant. It is because no one has taken responsibility for keeping it in view.

How Narratives Form

Narratives do not begin as stories.

They begin as shortcuts.

A system cannot hold every fact, every condition, every variable that shaped a person's behavior. So it compresses. It looks for patterns that feel explanatory enough to move forward. This is not corruption. It is efficiency. But efficiency has a cost, and that cost is usually paid by context.

Once context thins, narrative thickens.

A missed deadline does not stay a missed deadline for long. It becomes a data point. A delayed response becomes another. An organizational lapse joins them. Individually, these events might be explainable, even ordinary. Together, they begin to cohere into something that feels like insight.

Humans are pattern-making machines. Institutions are no different.

At some point, the system stops asking what happened here and starts asking what kind of person does this. That shift is subtle, but it is decisive. Behavior is no longer evaluated as situational. It is interpreted as dispositional. The question changes from "Why did this occur?" to "Who is this lawyer?" That is where narrative is born.

Narratives form because systems need continuity. They need a stable way to understand what they are seeing. Once a provisional explanation appears to fit, it gets reused. The brain loves reuse. Institutions love it even more.

This is how a working theory hardens into an identity.

What makes this especially dangerous for lawyers with ADHD is that many ADHD-related struggles are episodic, not constant. Performance is not uniformly impaired. It fluctuates. It improves dramatically under certain conditions and deteriorates under others. That variability confuses systems that expect linear output.

Instead of interpreting fluctuation as evidence of environmental sensitivity, the system often reads it as inconsistency. And inconsistency is one of the few traits the legal profession has almost no tolerance for.

From the outside, it looks like a simple conclusion. If someone can perform well sometimes, they should be able to perform well all the time. When they do not, the explanation feels obvious.

The explanation is often wrong. But once it is written into the narrative, it becomes difficult to dislodge. Narratives gain power because they reduce uncertainty. They allow evaluators to feel oriented. They allow decision-makers to move forward without revisiting first principles every time something goes wrong. The problem is that narratives are sticky. Once formed, they shape what the system notices next.

This is confirmation bias institutionalized.

New information is not evaluated neutrally. It is filtered. Evidence that supports the narrative is highlighted. Evidence that complicates it is minimized or explained away. Ambiguous behavior is resolved in the direction of the existing story.

A late filing becomes proof of unreliability rather than an isolated lapse. A missed call confirms disorganization rather than reflecting overload. Each new event does not stand alone. It accumulates.

What is especially pernicious is that positive performance often does not count against a negative narrative once it has formed. Good work is treated as an exception. A fluke. Something that happened despite the underlying issue, not evidence against it. This asymmetry matters.

For lawyers with ADHD, excellence often shows up in bursts. Trials. Hearings. High-stakes moments. Situations with urgency and immediacy. These moments demonstrate competence clearly and publicly. But they are episodic. Administrative work, long-term planning, and sustained routine are quieter, more fragile domains.

The system tends to weight quiet failures more heavily than visible successes when forming narratives, because failures feel diagnostic. The narrative becomes self-sealing.

Once this happens, the lawyer often senses the shift before it is ever articulated. Interactions change. Questions carry a different tone. Explanations are received with skepticism. The benefit of the doubt quietly disappears.

This is the psychological weight of narrative formation. It is not just about reputation. It is about trust. And trust, once withdrawn, is rarely restored by argument alone.

The cruel irony is that many lawyers respond to this shift by working harder in exactly the wrong way. They try to compensate through effort rather than redesign. They push longer hours. They rely more heavily on emergency mode. They compress margin even further in an attempt to prove reliability.

From the system's perspective, this often backfires. Increased strain produces more visible slippage. The narrative appears confirmed. From the inside, it feels like running uphill on loose gravel.

What the system does not see is the feedback loop it has created. Narrative shapes pressure. Pressure shapes performance. Performance then appears to validate the narrative. At no point does the system pause to ask whether its own interpretation is contributing to the outcome it is observing.

This is not because the system is hostile. It is because systems are not introspective by default.

Narratives are also seductive because they offer moral clarity. They turn complex behavior into something legible. They allow evaluators to feel justified. Once a narrative exists, decisions feel principled rather than contingent.

That sense of moral footing is difficult to surrender.

This is why simply "explaining ADHD" rarely works once a narrative has formed. The explanation arrives too late. The story has already been written in a language that does not include neurocognitive variability as a meaningful category.

To the system, the explanation sounds like an excuse because it does not map onto the narrative framework already in place.

Timing matters here.

Narratives are easiest to influence before they crystallize. Once they do, they resist revision. This is not unique to law. It is how human cognition works. First impressions anchor interpretation. Subsequent information adjusts around them rather than replacing them.

For lawyers with ADHD, this creates a narrow window where context must be made visible early and deliberately. Not after the fact. Not once the story has solidified. But while interpretation is still fluid.

That is uncomfortable advice, because it requires vulnerability before failure. It requires naming differences before they cause visible problems. It requires advocating for structure before the system believes it is necessary.

But the alternative is allowing the system to supply its own explanation.

And the system's explanations tend to be unkind.

Narratives also persist because they are rarely challenged internally. Institutions reward consensus. Once a shared understanding exists, questioning it feels disruptive. People do not want to be the one who reopens a settled story, especially if doing so introduces complexity.

Complexity slows things down. Systems dislike slowing down.

This is how narratives outlive the conditions that created them. A lawyer may change environments. Improve systems. Stabilize performance. But the narrative lingers. It colors interpretation long after its factual basis has weakened.

That lingering effect is one of the most psychologically damaging aspects of narrative formation. It creates a sense that no amount of improvement is sufficient. The bar keeps moving. The past keeps reappearing.

This is where identity erosion begins.

The lawyer starts to internalize the story the system is telling. Doubt creeps in. Confidence narrows. Risk tolerance drops. The very traits that once supported strong advocacy become harder to access.

None of this is visible on paper. All of it affects performance.

This is why narrative formation cannot be treated as a secondary issue. It is not merely reputational. It is structural. It shapes the conditions under which future behavior occurs.

The goal, then, is not to eliminate narratives. That is impossible. Humans and systems require them. The goal is to intervene before they harden into distortions.

That intervention starts with preserving context, but it does not end there. Context alone does not rewrite stories. It has to be framed in a way the system can process.

The next section turns to that problem directly. Not how to excuse behavior, but how to prevent misinterpretation from becoming destiny. Not how to fight narratives after they form, but how to slow their formation long enough to ensure they are accurate.

Because once a narrative replaces context, it rarely gives it back voluntarily.

And by the time it does, the damage is usually already done.

Why Proactive Clarity Matters

By the time a system is asking questions, the narrative is usually already in motion.

That is the part most people misunderstand. Institutions rarely begin with curiosity. They begin with pattern recognition. Something looks off. Something does not fit expectation. Something repeats. The system notices the deviation first and only later looks for an explanation. By then, the explanation is already constrained by the frame that has formed around the behavior.

Proactive clarity exists to interrupt that process before it hardens.

When context is absent, systems default to inference. When inference fills the gap, it almost always leans toward personal explanation rather than structural or neurological one. The behavior becomes the evidence. The pattern becomes the diagnosis. The story closes quickly because it feels coherent.

Proactive clarity does not mean oversharing. It does not mean apology. It does not mean preemptively defending yourself against a future accusation. It means making the relevant context visible early enough that it is incorporated into how behavior is understood, rather than introduced later as a complication.

There is a critical timing element here. Context offered after a narrative has formed sounds like excuse. Context offered before a narrative forms sounds like information. The content may be identical. The reception is not.

This is why waiting for a problem before explaining ADHD, executive function issues, or environmental constraints is so risky. Once a system believes it has identified a character issue, everything that follows is filtered through that belief. Missed deadlines confirm it. Delayed responses reinforce it. Even corrective action is interpreted as damage control rather than competence.

Proactive clarity changes the baseline.

When a system understands, in advance, how a person's brain works, what conditions support reliable performance, and where predictable friction points exist, the same behaviors are read differently. A delay is evaluated as a signal, not a verdict. A deviation prompts inquiry rather than assumption. The system still expects competence, but it no longer mistakes neurological variance for indifference.

This is not about lowering standards. It is about aligning expectations with reality.

In professions like law, where performance is evaluated largely through outcomes rather than process, clarity about process matters more than people realize. Two lawyers can produce the same result through very different internal paths.

One path fits the system's assumptions. The other does not. Without explanation, the system treats difference as defect.

Proactive clarity names the difference before it is misread.

It also creates a record. Not a defensive record, but a factual one. Documentation of diagnosis, accommodation requests, and structural supports does more than protect against future misunderstanding. It anchors interpretation. It makes it harder for later observers to strip behavior of context and assign motive where none exists.

This matters not because discipline is inevitable, but because misinterpretation is common. Most systems are not hostile. They are simplistic. They are built to move quickly, categorize efficiently, and resolve uncertainty with the least friction possible. That efficiency works well for the majority. It fails quietly for anyone whose cognition does not match the assumed template.

Clarity slows that failure down. It also changes how you relate to your own work. When context is named openly, the internal shame loop loses some of its power. You stop treating every friction point as a personal defect that must be hidden. You begin designing around reality instead of performing against it. That shift alone reduces cognitive load.

There is a difference between transparency and vulnerability. Proactive clarity is not emotional exposure. It is structural honesty. It says, "This is how my brain operates. These are the conditions under which I do my best work. These are the supports that allow consistency." It does not ask for indulgence. It sets parameters.

Systems respond better to parameters than to apologies.

None of this guarantees perfect understanding. It does not eliminate friction. It does not make every evaluator fair or every institution enlightened. What it does is prevent silence from doing the system's interpretive work for it. Silence invites assumption. Clarity limits it.

That is the real value.

When context is visible, narratives form differently. When narratives form differently, outcomes change. Not because the rules bend, but because they are applied with a fuller picture of the person standing inside them.

In a profession that prizes foresight, proactive clarity is not a concession. It is strategy.

And in a system that too often confuses behavior with character, it is one of the few ways to keep the story honest before it starts writing itself.

Part IV

What Changes When You See It Clearly

Chapter 15
Misreading Behavior
When Context is Treated as Irrelevant

Systems do not experience people the way other people do. They do not see effort, context, fatigue, or intent. They see patterns. And once a pattern forms, everything else gets filtered through it.

That is not a flaw unique to the legal profession. It is how large institutions function. They are designed to reduce complexity. They cannot hold nuance for very long. They rely on repetition, regularity, and predictability as stand-ins for reliability. When behavior fits those expectations, the system relaxes. When it does not, the system begins to search for an explanation.

The explanation is rarely neurological.

When context disappears, behavior does not remain neutral. It becomes evidence. A late filing is no longer just a late filing. It becomes part of a sequence. A missed response is no longer an isolated oversight. It becomes a data point. Over time, those data points begin to cluster, and the system does what it was built to do. It draws a line through them and calls it a story.

This is where lawyers with ADHD often lose control of the narrative without realizing it.

From the inside, the behavior feels familiar. Uneven focus. Bursts of intensity followed by administrative drag. Long stretches of competent, even excellent work punctuated by inexplicable gaps. None of this feels intentional. None of it feels reckless. It feels like working inside a nervous system that does not distribute energy evenly.

From the outside, it reads differently.

The system does not see the long nights, the hyperfocus, the preparation that went unseen because it did not leave a clean paper trail. It does not see the internal cost of getting back on track after a derailment. It sees output. Timing. Responsiveness. Compliance with expectations that assume a uniform relationship to attention and time.

Once the system begins reading behavior through that lens, it becomes very difficult to reinsert context. Explanations arrive too late. Nuance sounds like excuse. Variability starts to look like unreliability, even when the underlying performance tells a more complicated story.

This is not because the system is hostile. It is because the system is literal.

How the System Interprets Behavior Without Context

Once context disappears, the system does not pause. It does not wait for clarification. It does not mark the file "incomplete" and hold judgment in abeyance. It does what systems are designed to do. It interprets.

This is the part that is rarely examined because it feels neutral. Interpretation is treated as an objective act, a simple reading of observable behavior. A deadline was missed. A response was delayed. Communication was inconsistent. A pattern emerged. The system believes it is merely recording facts.

But interpretation is never neutral. It is shaped by the assumptions built into the structure doing the interpreting.

Legal systems are optimized for visible behavior, not internal process. They are built to measure outputs rather than conditions. Timeliness, responsiveness, orderliness, and consistency are treated as proxies for competence because they are easy to observe and easy to compare. They fit neatly into forms, checklists, timelines, and findings.

What the system does not measure is effort, strain, or cognitive load. It does not measure how much internal work was required to produce a given outcome. It does not measure how many starts preceded a finish, how many hours were spent circling a task before ignition, or how much energy was consumed simply trying to begin.

Once context is gone, those invisible variables do not remain neutral. They are replaced.

The system substitutes intention.

This is the critical move. When the system encounters behavior without explanation, it fills the gap with motive. A late filing becomes a choice rather than a constraint. An unanswered email becomes disregard rather than overload. Disorganization becomes carelessness rather than impairment. The absence of visible struggle is read as the absence of struggle itself.

This is not because the system is malicious. It is because the system is designed to read patterns, not causes.

Pattern recognition is one of the system's core functions. Courts, regulators, and disciplinary bodies rely on it to maintain consistency. Repeated behavior is treated as diagnostic. Isolated events are discounted. Trends are elevated. Over time, behavior is aggregated and given meaning.

The problem arises when the pattern itself is incomplete.

In ADHD, inconsistency is not random. It is state-dependent. Performance fluctuates based on urgency, environment, sensory load, emotional activation, and timing. The same lawyer can appear exceptionally capable in one context and inexplicably unreliable in another. When the system lacks the framework to understand that variability, it treats fluctuation as evidence of choice.

Consistency is mistaken for character. Inconsistency is mistaken for indifference.

Once that interpretive frame is in place, everything that follows is filtered through it. Subsequent behavior is not assessed on its own terms. It is evaluated in light of the narrative already forming. Each data point becomes confirmation rather than information.

This is how narratives harden.

The system does not ask, "What conditions produced this outcome?" It asks, "What does this pattern say about this person?" The answer to that question feels logical, even inevitable, because the system has already removed the variables that would complicate it.

What looks like judgment is often just momentum.

Another quiet substitution happens at the same time. Capacity is conflated with availability. Because a lawyer has demonstrated high-level performance under certain conditions, the system assumes that performance should be available at all times. The fact that the performance depended on urgency, structure, or external scaffolding disappears. What remains is the expectation.

This is where ADHD lawyers are often misunderstood most profoundly. Their best work becomes the baseline against which all work is measured. When they cannot replicate that level of output in a low-stimulus, high-administration environment, the system reads the difference as decline rather than context shift.

The question the system never asks is whether the environment changed the task.

Instead, it asks why the lawyer did not maintain the same level of performance.

This interpretive shortcut feels reasonable because it mirrors how the system evaluates everyone else. The problem is that the baseline assumption is wrong. It assumes uniform access to executive function across settings. It assumes time is experienced evenly. It assumes initiation is a matter of will.

Those assumptions are invisible because they are shared by the people building and enforcing the system.

Once misinterpretation takes hold, corrective signals are often misread as well. A lawyer working harder under strain may appear more chaotic, not more diligent. Increased effort without corresponding output is interpreted as inefficiency rather than impairment. Attempts to compensate can look like escalation rather than adaptation.

The system is not trained to distinguish between struggle and resistance.

This is why explanations offered late in the process rarely land. By the time a lawyer tries to reintroduce context, the interpretive frame is already set. The system hears the explanation not as missing information, but as justification. The story has moved on. The explanation arrives too late to change its direction.

From the system's perspective, this feels fair. Everyone is being held to the same standard. Everyone is being evaluated on observable conduct. Uniform rules are being applied uniformly.

What the system does not see is that uniform application of standards does not produce uniform impact.

The misreading of behavior is not an aberration. It is the predictable outcome of a system that values legibility over accuracy. Legible behavior is easier to regulate. Complex explanations slow the process down. Context complicates enforcement. The system selects for clarity even when clarity distorts reality.

This is why misinterpretation persists even in the face of contrary evidence. It is not that the system refuses to understand. It is that understanding is not what the system is optimized to do.

Once behavior is misread, the consequences follow naturally. Intervention escalates. Oversight increases. Flexibility decreases. The environment becomes more rigid at the precise moment when rigidity makes performance harder. The system believes it is correcting a problem. In reality, it is amplifying it.

None of this requires bad faith. It requires only incomplete information and a structure that treats interpretation as fact.

This section matters because it reframes the problem. The issue is not that lawyers with ADHD fail to meet expectations. It is that expectations are formed through a lens that cannot see how performance actually works.

When behavior is stripped of context and read through assumptions that do not apply, misinterpretation is not an exception. It is the rule.

Understanding that does not excuse mistakes. It explains why the same mistakes keep being misunderstood in the same way.

And once you see that pattern, the next question becomes unavoidable: how do you prevent the system from filling the silence with the wrong story?

That question is where the chapter turns next.

How Narratives Form & Why They Are So Hard to Undo

Once behavior has been misread, the system does not remain tentative about it. Interpretation quickly becomes narrative.

This shift is subtle, but decisive. Interpretation asks what something might mean. Narrative declares what it does mean.

At that point, behavior is no longer being evaluated in isolation. It is being fitted into a story that explains past events and predicts future ones.

Narratives form because systems need coherence. They need a throughline that allows disparate facts to make sense together. A missed deadline, a delayed response, an incomplete filing, and an eventual correction are messy on their own. As a group, they invite explanation. The system supplies one.

The explanation is rarely framed as accusation. It is framed as assessment. A pattern emerges. Reliability is questioned. Judgment is discussed. Professionalism becomes the lens.

Once that lens is in place, new information is not weighed neutrally. It is filtered.

This is where the process becomes self-reinforcing. Facts that align with the narrative are emphasized. Facts that complicate it are minimized or dismissed as anomalies. Improvement is treated as temporary. Success is treated as exception. Failure is treated as confirmation.

The system tends to treat quiet failures as more revealing than visible successes, because failures feel diagnostic. A strong performance can be explained away as luck, assistance, or circumstance. A lapse, by contrast, is treated as a glimpse of the "real" issue. The narrative sharpens around what went wrong, not what went right.

This dynamic is especially punishing for ADHD lawyers, whose performance naturally varies by context. High-functioning periods are discounted because they disrupt the story the system is telling. Inconsistent performance is not seen as evidence of state-dependence. It is seen as proof of instability.

At that point, intent becomes irrelevant.

The narrative does not ask whether the lawyer meant to comply, cared about the obligation, or worked intensely to correct the issue. Those questions belong to an earlier stage, before the story hardened. Now the system is tracking reliability, not effort.

This is why late explanations struggle to gain traction. Once a narrative exists, explanations are interpreted through it. They are no longer information. They are defense.

A lawyer who tries to explain cognitive load or executive dysfunction after a narrative has formed is often heard as minimizing responsibility rather than adding context. The system assumes that if the explanation were legitimate, it would have appeared earlier. The fact that it appears now becomes part of the story itself.

This creates a structural disadvantage that is difficult to overcome. ADHD-related impairments are often invisible until stress accumulates. By the time consequences surface, the opportunity to shape the narrative has already passed.

Narratives also gain authority through repetition. The same description appears in multiple documents. Language hardens. Phrases are reused. Observations are copied forward. Over time, the narrative takes on the weight of fact simply because it has been recorded so many times.

What began as interpretation becomes institutional memory.

Once that happens, even neutral actors inherit the story. A new reviewer, supervisor, or decision-maker encounters the narrative fully formed. They are not starting from scratch. They are stepping into a file that already tells them who this person is.

The system rarely asks whether the narrative itself was shaped by missing information. It assumes that if the story exists, it must have been earned.

This is how behavior becomes identity.

An inconsistency becomes unreliability. A lapse becomes neglect. A struggle becomes a trait. The system stops responding to events and starts responding to the person it believes those events reveal.

At that stage, corrective actions often backfire. Increased oversight is interpreted as necessary control. Requests for flexibility are seen as resistance. Efforts to explain feel defensive. Silence feels like confirmation.

The narrative leaves very little room to move.

This is not unique to ADHD, but ADHD makes it more likely because the system is not calibrated to recognize state-dependent performance. When variability is treated as defect, the story writes itself.

The tragedy is that many of these narratives are preventable. They form not because the lawyer is incapable, but because the system never learned how to read the signals it was receiving. Once the wrong story is in place, the cost of correcting it rises exponentially.

Understanding how narratives form is essential because it shifts the focus from individual incidents to structural dynamics.

The problem is not a single missed deadline or a single delayed response. The problem is how those events are woven together and what the system assumes they mean.

This is also why proactive clarity matters. Once a narrative has formed, clarity feels like excuse. Before it forms, clarity feels like information.

That difference is everything.

The next section turns to that distinction, and to why timing matters as much as substance when it comes to being understood by a system that prefers clean stories to complicated truths.

When Behavior Becomes a Proxy for Character

Once context disappears and narratives harden, the system does something subtle but devastating. It stops describing behavior and starts inferring character.

This is the pivot point where misunderstanding becomes damage.

A missed deadline stops being a data point and becomes evidence. A delayed response stops being a symptom and becomes a trait. A period of inconsistency stops being situational and starts to feel diagnostic. The system does not say this out loud, but it acts on it all the same. The story shifts from what happened to what kind of lawyer this must be.

That shift is rarely intentional. It happens because systems are built to simplify. They cannot hold complexity for long. They want coherence. And the easiest form of coherence is moral.

So behavior gets translated. Slippage becomes neglect. Disorganization becomes irresponsibility. Inconsistency becomes unreliability. The translation happens quietly, without malice, and almost always without awareness that anything has been lost in the process.

For lawyers with ADHD, this is where things go wrong fast.

ADHD produces variability. Not randomness, but unevenness. Strong performance under urgency. Weaker performance in low-stimulus environments. Bursts of clarity followed by periods of friction. This variability is neurological, predictable, and well-documented. But systems built around linear performance models do not know what to do with it. They expect smoothness. When they see oscillation, they reach for explanations that fit their framework.

Character is the most available explanation.

Once that happens, everything else gets reinterpreted through that lens. Prior successes are reframed as luck or effort spikes. Future struggles are seen as confirmation. Neutral events start to feel suspicious. The record begins to tilt.

What makes this especially dangerous is that the system often believes it is being fair.

It points to the behavior and says, "We are responding to what we see." It insists that standards are neutral, that expectations are uniform, that outcomes speak for themselves. But outcomes never speak alone. They are always interpreted. And interpretation is shaped by what the system is prepared to see.

ADHD behavior does not look like impairment to a system trained to recognize only two categories: compliance and misconduct. There is no slot for "functionally capable, but context-sensitive." There is no checkbox for "performs best under urgency." There is no column for "requires external structure to maintain consistency."

So the system fills the gap with judgment.

This is how a lawyer who is trusted in court can be doubted in chambers. How someone praised for trial work can be criticized for follow-through. How a person known as sharp, prepared, and effective can slowly acquire a reputation for being "hard to manage" or "unreliable," without any single event justifying that conclusion.

The behavior never changed. The story did.

Once character enters the narrative, the system stops asking operational questions. It stops asking what supports might help, what structures are missing, what conditions produced the lapse. Those questions belong to a functional analysis. Character analysis does not need them.

Character analysis only needs patterns.

And this is where ADHD becomes invisible again. The system believes it is identifying a pattern of conduct, when what it is actually seeing is a pattern of friction between a brain and an environment that was never designed for it.

There is a particular cruelty in this for lawyers, because the profession equates reliability with trustworthiness. If you cannot be counted on in administrative moments, the inference is that you cannot be counted on at all. The leap is illogical, but it feels intuitive to people who have never experienced executive function impairment.

What gets lost is the reality that reliability is not a single trait. It is domain-specific. A lawyer can be profoundly reliable in moments that require judgment, advocacy, and presence, while struggling in moments that require sustained, low-stimulation execution. The system does not distinguish between these domains. It treats them as interchangeable expressions of the same underlying quality. They are not.

This is why the system often reacts more harshly to quiet failures than visible ones. A dramatic mistake in court is contextualized. Everyone was there. Pressure was obvious. Stakes were clear. A missed filing deadline in the office has no visible pressure attached to it. It looks simple. Which makes it easier to moralize.

The irony is that the quieter the failure, the louder the judgment.

And once that judgment takes hold, it becomes self-reinforcing. The lawyer senses the shift. Trust feels thinner. Scrutiny feels sharper. Anxiety increases. Executive function degrades further. The behavior the system is worried about becomes more likely, not less.

From the inside, this feels like sliding downhill on ice. The harder you try to stand still, the faster you move.

This is the moment where many lawyers internalize the system's story. They start to believe that the inconsistency means something about who they are. They stop advocating for context because context has already been dismissed. They focus on hiding symptoms instead of addressing them. They work harder, longer, and more silently, hoping effort will substitute for structure.

Sometimes it does, for a while. But effort is not a sustainable accommodation.

The tragedy here is not that the system enforces standards. Standards matter. The tragedy is that the system mistakes how someone struggles for why they struggle, and then treats the misinterpretation as truth.

Behavior becomes character. Character becomes destiny. And none of that was necessary.

If the system paused long enough to separate impairment from intent, variability from unreliability, friction from indifference, the story would change. Not to one of excuse, but to one of accuracy. The response would shift from punishment to design. From judgment to adjustment.

That shift does not lower the bar. It clarifies it.

This section matters because it names the moment where misunderstanding hardens into consequence. Once you see that moment, you can intervene earlier. You can insist on context before conclusions. You can document before narratives form. You can refuse to let your work be reduced to a caricature of its hardest moments. The system misreads behavior because it was never taught how to read anything else.

Seeing that clearly is not an indictment of the profession. It is an invitation to do better.

Chapter 16
Making the Invisible Visible
How Context Disappears and Why It Matters

For a long time, I thought the problem was that I wasn't seeing myself clearly enough.

I assumed that if I could just become more self-aware, more disciplined, more organized, more vigilant, everything would stabilize. When something slipped, I went looking inward. When I struggled to start, I interrogated my motivation. When exhaustion showed up without explanation, I treated it like a personal weakness I hadn't yet overcome.

That reflex was not accidental. It was learned.

Early in my practice, I handled a case that should have been routine. Nothing novel. Nothing dramatic. A short hearing, a manageable client, familiar law. I prepared the way I always did. I knew the file. I knew the arguments. I walked into court steady and focused, did the work, answered the questions, and walked back into the hallway with that quiet sense of relief that comes from things going as they should.

By any external measure, the morning was a success.

When I got back to the office, I sat down at my desk intending to finish what I had put off for the hearing. Emails. A short draft. Administrative clean-up. The kind of work that usually waits patiently while court takes precedence.

Nothing moved.

I opened documents I had already read. I reread emails without responding. I stared at a screen that should have felt familiar and felt nothing but resistance. The clarity I had in court was gone. Not diminished. Gone. I remember thinking, This doesn't make sense. I was just functioning at a high level.

So I did what the profession teaches you to do. I blamed myself.

I told myself I had lost focus. That I was being careless. That I should have more stamina than this. I stayed later than I needed to, not because the work required it, but because I felt I had to compensate for something I couldn't explain. I left the office tired, frustrated, and quietly ashamed—despite having done exactly what was asked of me that day.

What I did not consider was whether the cost of the morning had followed me back into the afternoon.

I did not have language for what had happened. I did not understand that court had demanded sustained regulation— attention, timing, restraint, emotional control—and that I had paid that cost in full while I was there. I did not understand that nothing about the legal system assumes that cost continues to exist once you leave the courtroom. The hearing ended. The ruling was entered. The system considered the matter closed.

My nervous system did not.

At the time, I treated the disconnect as a failure of character. In hindsight, it was a failure of visibility.

This book has spent the last several chapters naming things the profession routinely ignores: invisible labor, cognitive debt, distorted time perception, initiation friction, emotional carryover. Those concepts matter, but they are not abstract. They show up in ordinary days like this one—days that look successful from the outside and quietly destabilizing from the inside.

Making the invisible visible is not about vindication. It is about accuracy.

When effort, depletion, and regulation are hidden, behavior becomes the only thing the system can see. And when behavior is all that is visible, it is inevitably misread. Delay becomes indifference. Inconsistency becomes unreliability. Fatigue becomes lack of discipline. The story writes itself long before anyone asks whether it is true.

The most damaging part of that process is not how the system responds. It is how quickly lawyers learn to adopt the same misinterpretation about themselves.

This chapter is about interrupting that reflex.

Not by offering solutions, and not by asking for sympathy, but by insisting on a fuller picture of what is actually happening when an ADHD brain moves through a profession that was never designed to notice how much work happens beneath the surface.

Once that picture is visible, responsibility does not disappear. It becomes intelligible. And that changes everything that follows.

Most failures in the legal profession do not begin as failures at all. They begin as ordinary behavior, interpreted without context.

A missed deadline is read as carelessness. A delayed response becomes indifference. Inconsistent performance is taken as unreliability. None of those conclusions require malice. They require only one assumption: that everyone experiences work, time, and pressure in roughly the same way.

That assumption is wrong.

What this book has traced, chapter by chapter, is not a story of incapacity, but a story of mismatch. A brain that performs exceptionally under certain conditions is judged almost exclusively under conditions where its strengths are least visible. When the system encounters friction, it looks inward, not outward. It examines the lawyer's behavior, not the environment shaping it. It evaluates outcomes without asking how those outcomes were produced.

This is not because the system is cruel. It is because it is incomplete.

Legal culture prizes clarity, predictability, and consistency. Those values make sense. Clients deserve reliability. Courts require order. The public expects competence. But the profession has quietly collapsed "competence" into a narrow set of surface behaviors, many of which are administrative, repetitive, and temporally abstract. When those behaviors falter, the explanation defaults to character.

What is missing from that analysis is visibility.

The internal mechanics of ADHD—time distortion, delayed activation, state-dependent focus, emotional load—are largely invisible to outsiders. They leave no obvious trace until something slips. By the time the system notices, the only evidence available is the slip itself. Context has already vanished.

This is the danger zone.

Once behavior is separated from the conditions that produced it, narratives harden quickly. A pattern is inferred. Intent is assumed. Explanations offered later are treated as rationalizations rather than information. At that point, even accurate descriptions of disability can sound like excuses, not because they are wrong, but because they arrive too late.

The problem, then, is not that the system refuses to understand ADHD. The problem is that it does not see it soon enough.

This chapter is about preventing that disappearance. Not through confrontation. Not through disclosure as confession. But through clarity—clear structures, clear records, clear boundaries that make invisible labor legible before misunderstanding takes root.

Competence does not require sameness. It requires that the system see what it is actually evaluating.

That is where the work turns next.

When Explanation Comes Too Late

The most dangerous moment for any professional is not the mistake itself. It is the moment after the mistake has already been interpreted.

Once behavior has been labeled, explanation loses power. Context sounds defensive. Nuance feels like backpedaling. Even accurate descriptions of what happened are filtered through a narrative that has already settled in place. This is not unique to law, but the legal profession is particularly unforgiving about it because we are trained to believe that timing is everything.

By the time a lawyer with ADHD is asked to explain a lapse, the explanation is already suspect. That is not because the explanation lacks merit. It is because it arrives after the system believes it has seen enough.

I learned this the hard way. Not in one dramatic moment, but through a series of smaller realizations that accumulated over time. I would explain how something slipped. I would describe the workload, the compression, the environmental factors, the way time collapsed or activation failed. The explanation would be met with polite acknowledgment, followed by a return to the same conclusion. The explanation did not change the interpretation because the interpretation was already complete.

From the system's perspective, this makes sense. Lawyers are expected to anticipate problems, not explain them afterward. We are trained to believe that foresight is a measure of competence. So when foresight appears to fail, the system assumes a failure of responsibility rather than a failure of perception.

What the system does not see is that for many ADHD lawyers, the failure is not foresight, but timing. The signals that would have prompted earlier action never arrived. The cost of delay did not register until it was too late to avoid it. The work may have been happening the entire time, just not in a way that produced visible reassurance.

That invisibility is what makes reactive explanation so fragile.

When a lawyer says, "Here is why this happened," what the system often hears is, "Here is why I should not be held accountable." Even when that is not the intent, even when the explanation is offered in good faith, it collides with a professional culture that values prevention over explanation.

This is why so many lawyers with ADHD hesitate to disclose or contextualize their experience at all. They sense, often correctly, that explaining after the fact can make things worse. Silence feels safer than a story that might be misread as excuse-making.

The result is a quiet trap. You do not explain early because nothing has gone wrong yet. You do not explain late because the explanation will not be believed. Somewhere in the middle, the opportunity disappears.

The system is not hostile to explanation. It is hostile to surprise.

What it rewards is predictability. What it punishes is deviation it did not see coming. That distinction matters, because it shifts the goal. The goal is not to justify behavior after it has been judged. The goal is to prevent misinterpretation before judgment forms.

That requires a different approach.

Reactive explanation asks the system to revise a story it has already told itself. Proactive clarity prevents the wrong story from forming in the first place. It makes the invisible visible early, when it still reads as information rather than defense.

This is not about oversharing or preemptive confession. It is about reducing ambiguity. When ambiguity exists, the system fills it in with familiar assumptions. Those assumptions rarely favor neurological difference.

Once you understand that, the strategy changes. The question is no longer, "How do I explain myself if something goes wrong?" The question becomes, "How do I make my working reality legible before anyone needs an explanation?"

That is where leverage lives.

Making the Invisible Legible

Proactive clarity is not about predicting failure. It is about reducing ambiguity before the system is forced to interpret behavior on its own.

Most institutional misreadings begin in silence. Not intentional silence, not deception, just the ordinary absence of explanation that exists when nothing appears to be wrong. Work is getting done. The wheels are turning. There is no reason to narrate the process. Until there is.

The problem is that the legal system does not evaluate internal process. It evaluates artifacts. Filings. Responses.

Appearances. Timelines. When those artifacts arrive late, incomplete, or compressed, the system does not ask what happened inside the work. It asks what kind of lawyer produces outcomes like this.

Proactive clarity changes the raw material the system works with.

It does not require disclosure of diagnosis. It does not require vulnerability speeches or medical explanations. It requires something far more practical: advance signaling about how work is structured, where friction points exist, and how those points are being managed.

In other words, it turns private reality into shared expectation.

I did not understand this early in my career. I assumed professionalism meant absorbing friction quietly. I believed that competence meant handling difficulties without drawing attention to them. I thought that explaining how I worked would make me sound disorganized or incapable. So I stayed quiet and trusted results to speak for themselves.

That works only when results are smooth.

The moment results compress, silence becomes interpretive space. And the system does not leave interpretive space empty.

Proactive clarity fills that space with context before it becomes narrative.

In practice, this looks unremarkable. It sounds like ordinary communication, except it arrives earlier and with more intention. A brief note that a filing will be submitted closer to the deadline because preparation is ongoing. A calendar reset that acknowledges compression instead of pretending it does not exist. A conversation that frames pace as deliberate rather than reactive.

None of this announces weakness. It establishes predictability.

Predictability is the currency institutions trust most. When people know what to expect, deviation feels manageable. When they do not, deviation feels like risk.

For a lawyer with ADHD, predictability cannot always come from internal timing. It has to be externalized. That externalization is not just for personal function. It is for institutional legibility.

The system is far more tolerant of delay it can see coming than delay it experiences as surprise. The same outcome reads differently depending on whether it arrives with explanation or without it.

This is why proactive clarity must happen upstream. Once a delay occurs without context, the explanation that follows feels like repair. Repair always carries suspicion.

Upstream clarity reframes the work as intentional rather than erratic.

There is also a second benefit that is easy to miss. Proactive clarity reduces internal pressure. When you are not carrying the burden of invisibility, you are not constantly managing the fear of being misread. That fear drains cognitive resources that are already in short supply. Making your process legible frees attention for the work itself.

This does not mean narrating every difficulty. It means identifying the predictable friction points and addressing them in advance. Time compression. Activation delays. Environmental constraints. Workload clustering. These are not personal failures. They are known features of how the work gets done.

Naming them early makes them less dramatic later.

The mistake many lawyers make is assuming that silence preserves reputation. In reality, silence allows others to construct explanations on your behalf. Those explanations tend to default toward character rather than circumstance.

Proactive clarity does not ask the system to lower standards. It asks the system to understand how standards are being met.

That distinction matters.

When the system understands the process, outcomes are evaluated in proportion. When it does not, outcomes are treated as evidence of something deeper and more concerning than they often are.

This is the difference between being assessed and being misread.

The goal is not immunity. The goal is accuracy.

Once you understand that, proactive clarity stops feeling like exposure and starts feeling like control. You are not waiting to be explained. You are shaping the frame through which your work is seen.

That is not indulgence. It is professional self-preservation.

And it is the only reliable way to keep context from disappearing when it matters most.

When Legibility Arrives Too Late

There is a moment in every professional story when the explanation stops mattering.

It is not because the explanation is wrong. It is because the system has already decided what it is seeing. Once that decision hardens, new information no longer functions as context. It functions as excuse. And the difference between the two is not substance. It is timing.

This is where most lawyers misunderstand what goes wrong.

They assume that if they can eventually explain themselves clearly enough, the system will recalibrate. That if they can just show how the behavior made sense in context, the record will soften. That if they are sincere, reasonable, and cooperative, the narrative will reopen.

It rarely does.

Systems do not revise stories easily. They finalize them.

By the time context is offered defensively, it is already competing with something more powerful than facts: pattern recognition. Human systems are built to spot repetition and draw conclusions from it. When they see missed deadlines, compressed communication, inconsistent responsiveness, or uneven administrative output, they do not wait to be educated. They fill in the blanks themselves.

And once those blanks are filled, they tend to stay filled.

This is why good lawyers are often blindsided by how quickly trust erodes when something slips. From the inside, the lapse feels isolated. From the outside, it looks like confirmation. The system is not tracking effort, intention, or internal strain. It is tracking visible behavior across time. When that behavior lacks context, the system supplies its own.

That is how competence gets quietly reclassified as risk.

What makes this especially dangerous for lawyers with ADHD is that the behaviors most likely to be misread are also the ones most likely to appear under stress. When executive function falters, output becomes uneven. When time perception distorts, responsiveness compresses. When cognitive load spikes, communication narrows. None of this reflects a loss of skill. It reflects a predictable neurological response to pressure.

But the system does not read neurology. It reads outcomes.

By the time the lawyer realizes how they are being seen, the story is often already written. The explanation arrives late, after concern has calcified into conclusion. At that point, even accurate context sounds like revisionism. The system hears it not as clarification, but as resistance.

This is the quiet cost of illegibility.

It is not punishment. It is drift.

Drift is what happens when no one intervenes early enough to name what is actually happening. It is how minor inconsistencies accumulate meaning they were never meant to carry. It is how a capable lawyer becomes "unreliable" without ever deciding to be. It is how behavior untethered from explanation starts to define identity.

Once drift sets in, everything becomes harder.

Every delay is read through the same lens. Every request for flexibility is scrutinized. Every explanation is weighed against a story that already exists. The system does not need to be hostile for this to happen. It only needs to be incomplete.

That is why proactive clarity matters more than perfect performance.

The goal is not to eliminate every symptom or smooth every rough edge. That is neither realistic nor necessary. The goal is to make sure that when the system observes your behavior, it has the correct framework for interpreting it. That framework has to exist before pressure distorts the surface. Once the surface cracks, it is too late to install the foundation underneath.

This is not about over-disclosure or preemptive defense. It is about alignment. When expectations, structures, and explanations are in place early, behavior is read accurately. When they are not, behavior becomes the only data point the system trusts.

And behavior, stripped of context, tells a misleading story.

The tragedy is that none of this requires bad faith. No one has to be unfair for the outcome to be unjust. The system simply does what systems do. It simplifies. It categorizes. It reduces complexity to something manageable.

If you do not participate in shaping that simplification, it will happen without you.

That is the final risk this chapter is meant to surface. Not discipline. Not failure. Not collapse. Misinterpretation. The slow replacement of truth with narrative because the truth never arrived in time.

What comes next is not about blame or reform. It is about strategy. About how to make your work legible before stress obscures it. About how to ensure that when the system looks at you, it sees the right story, not the easiest one.

That is where the work continues.

Chapter 17
What this Book Is
Really About

This book was never about fixing ADHD.

It was not written to offer discipline strategies, productivity systems, or a new way to "try harder." It was not meant to reassure anyone that everything would be fine if they just learned to manage themselves better. And it was certainly not written to excuse mistakes or explain away responsibility.

This book was written to tell the truth about misalignment.

From the outside, the legal profession looks like a neutral proving ground. Same rules. Same deadlines. Same expectations. Same standard for everyone. The assumption is that if you are capable, diligent, and ethical, your performance should be stable across time and context. When it is not, the explanation defaults to character. Effort. Motivation. Care.

What this book has shown, chapter by chapter, is that this assumption is wrong.

The ADHD mind is not unreliable. It is context-sensitive. It responds differently to urgency, stimulation, clarity, consequence, and structure. It performs exceptionally well under some conditions and struggles under others, not because the lawyer changes, but because the environment does. When the profession treats those shifts as moral failings instead of predictable neurological responses, it misreads what it is seeing.

That misreading carries real consequences.

It creates shame where there should be understanding. It creates discipline where there should be design. It creates narratives of decline where there is often nothing more than mismatch. Over time, it convinces capable lawyers that their difficulty is personal rather than structural, internal rather than contextual.

This book was written to interrupt that story.

Not to deny responsibility, but to locate it accurately. Not to lower standards, but to question whether the standards are being applied with any understanding of how minds actually work. Not to argue that ADHD lawyers are fragile or doomed, but to make clear that success and failure in this profession are not solely the product of willpower.

If there is one idea that runs through every chapter, it is this: performance does not exist in isolation. It emerges from the interaction between a mind and the conditions surrounding it. When those conditions are hostile to how a brain initiates, sustains, or organizes work, the outcome will reflect that hostility, no matter how committed the lawyer may be.

This book is about learning to see that interaction clearly.

Once you do, many of the things that once felt like personal defects begin to look like signals. Not excuses. Signals. And signals, when properly understood, are not something to hide from. They are something to design around.

That is the ground this book has been standing on all along.

What Changes When You See It Clearly

Once you understand that performance is contextual, not moral, the entire landscape shifts.

You stop asking why you are inconsistent and start asking where you are consistent. You stop interrogating your character and start examining conditions. You stop treating every struggle as evidence of personal failure and start recognizing patterns that repeat for a reason. That change is not subtle. It is foundational.

Most lawyers are taught to internalize everything. If something goes wrong, look inward. Fix yourself. Tighten up. Be better. That reflex is so deeply ingrained that questioning it can feel irresponsible. But what this book has shown is that exclusive inward focus can be just as dangerous as denial. When all explanation lives inside the individual, the environment escapes scrutiny entirely.

Seeing clearly means noticing what actually changes your performance.

Urgency sharpens focus. Ambiguity stalls it. Immediate consequence activates action. Distant consequence fades. Clear structure lowers resistance. Undefined tasks increase it. High-stakes interaction brings clarity. Quiet, unstructured isolation often does not. These are not quirks. They are consistent neurological responses that appear again and again throughout this book.

Once you see that, shame loses much of its grip.

Shame thrives on confusion. It tells you that you should be able to do what others do in the same way they do it. It tells you that failure to do so is evidence of deficiency. But when the pattern becomes visible, shame stops making sense. The issue was never effort alone. It was fit.

This clarity does not make you passive. It makes you strategic.

You begin to design your practice instead of reacting to it. You stop relying on hope and start building structure. You lower activation barriers instead of waiting for motivation. You create artificial urgency where real urgency is absent. You externalize executive function rather than demanding it appear on command. You protect margin because you understand how quickly it disappears. You learn when to say no not out of fear, but out of accuracy.

Most importantly, you stop confusing accommodation with weakness.

The legal profession often treats accommodation as indulgence, something granted reluctantly to those who cannot keep up. This book has argued the opposite. Accommodation is precision. It is an acknowledgment that different brains require different scaffolding to reach the same substantive standard. It does not dilute competence. It makes competence accessible.

Seeing clearly also changes how you interpret other people.

Judges, colleagues, clients, and regulators often respond to behavior without understanding its source. When you understand the mechanics beneath your own performance, you are less likely to accept their narratives uncritically. You can respond with context instead of collapse. You can explain patterns instead of apologizing for them. You can advocate for structure instead of absorbing blame.

This does not guarantee understanding. The system does not change simply because you see it differently. But clarity gives you leverage. It allows you to engage deliberately rather than defensively. It lets you document, plan, and protect yourself before a story forms without you.

Seeing clearly does not eliminate risk. It changes where you put your energy.

Instead of fighting yourself, you begin to work with how your mind actually functions. Instead of hoping the environment will cooperate, you shape what you can. Instead of internalizing every struggle, you recognize when a system is asking something unreasonable of your wiring.

That shift is not just practical. It is stabilizing.

Because once you see what is really happening, you stop mistaking friction for failure. And that alone changes how you move forward.

What Responsibility Actually Requires

Responsibility is one of the most abused words in this entire conversation. It is invoked constantly and examined almost never. When things go wrong, responsibility is treated as self-evident, a moral lever pulled to justify consequences rather than a concept worth defining with care.

In the legal profession, responsibility is usually framed as a personal attribute. You are responsible because you hold a license. You are responsible because clients depend on you. You are responsible because the system says so. That framing sounds sensible until you look closely at what it assumes. It assumes that everyone enters the profession with the same cognitive tools, the same access to support, the same internal regulators, and the same capacity to function under identical conditions. It assumes uniformity where none exists.

The ADA rejected that assumption decades ago.

Responsibility, properly understood, does not disappear in the presence of disability. It changes shape. It requires different inputs. It demands different safeguards. It asks different questions at the outset so that failures are not misread at the end.

A lawyer with ADHD is not asking to be relieved of responsibility. They are asking for responsibility to be evaluated honestly. That means acknowledging that some failures arise not from disregard, but from predictable friction between a brain and a system that was never designed with that brain in mind. It means recognizing that responsibility includes the duty to request accommodation, but it also includes the duty of institutions to engage with those requests in good faith.

Too often, the profession treats accommodation as a favor instead of what it actually is: a mechanism for ensuring competence. When systems are adjusted so that executive function impairments are supported rather than punished, the quality of lawyering improves. Deadlines are met more reliably. Communication stabilizes. Errors decrease. Clients are better served. None of this is theoretical. It is observable wherever accommodation is taken seriously.

What undermines responsibility is not accommodation. What undermines responsibility is pretending that structure does not matter, context does not matter, and cognition does not matter. That pretense allows systems to offload their own design failures onto individuals and call the result accountability.

There is a quieter truth here, one that the profession rarely articulates. Many lawyers with ADHD have been carrying more responsibility, not less, for most of their careers. They compensate constantly. They over-prepare in visible arenas to offset vulnerabilities in invisible ones. They build private systems to survive public expectations. They absorb shame that does not belong to them because it feels easier than challenging the story being told about them.

That kind of compensatory responsibility is unsustainable. Eventually something gives. When it does, the system points to the moment of collapse and ignores the years of adaptation that preceded it. That is not an honest assessment of responsibility. It is selective memory.

Real responsibility requires proportionality. It requires asking whether the expectations placed on a lawyer are achievable under the conditions imposed. It requires distinguishing between unwillingness and inability, between neglect and impairment, between risk created by indifference and risk created by misalignment. Those distinctions are not soft. They are precise. They are the difference between discipline that protects the public and discipline that merely enforces conformity.

None of this excuses harm. Clients must be protected. Courts must function. Deadlines matter. But protection does not require blindness. Function does not require denial. The profession can hold lawyers accountable while also acknowledging that accountability must be tethered to reality.

If there is one corrective move the legal system needs to make, it is this: stop treating behavior as self-explanatory. Behavior is the surface. Responsibility lives underneath, shaped by cognition, environment, support, and design. When those factors are ignored, responsibility becomes a blunt instrument instead of a guiding principle.

This book has never argued for leniency. It argues for accuracy.

Accuracy in how we understand the ADHD mind. Accuracy in how we interpret behavior. Accuracy in how we assign meaning to mistakes. Accuracy in how we decide when discipline is appropriate and when accommodation is the legally required first step.

Responsibility does not mean pretending everyone is the same. It means taking differences seriously enough to respond to them intelligently. That is not a threat to the profession. It is the only way the profession remains worthy of the authority it holds.

Section III ends here because this is the pivot point. Once responsibility is reframed correctly, the final question becomes unavoidable: what we do with that understanding going forward. That is where the conclusion must land.

What Comes After Seeing Clearly

Once you see the pattern, you cannot unsee it. That is the final burden and the final gift of clarity. You recognize how often behavior has been mistaken for intent, how often outcomes have been judged without reference to conditions, how often people have been disciplined for symptoms that were never properly named. From that point forward, neutrality is no longer an option.

This is where many systems stall. Insight is acknowledged, nodded at, perhaps even praised, and then quietly set aside. The structure remains the same. The incentives remain the same. The stories remain the same. Nothing actually changes. That is not progress. It is deferral.

What comes after seeing clearly is choice.

For individual lawyers with ADHD, the choice is whether to continue absorbing the system's misunderstandings as personal failure or to begin asserting a more accurate narrative about how they work. That does not require confrontation for its own sake. It requires documentation, foresight, and a willingness to name needs before a crisis forces the issue. It requires abandoning the hope that excellence alone will protect you from misinterpretation. It often does not.

For institutions, the choice is more uncomfortable. It means deciding whether accountability will be grounded in realism or ritual. Whether discipline will be preceded by inquiry or simply justified by outcome. Whether the profession is serious about disability law when the subject is one of its own.

Nothing in this book requires lowering standards. It requires raising them. A system that prides itself on precision should not tolerate lazy explanations for complex behavior. A profession built on evidence should not cling to assumptions when better information is available. A discipline process that claims legitimacy should not operate as though context were irrelevant.

There is also a quieter implication here, one that does not announce itself but matters deeply. Many lawyers with ADHD are not struggling because they are fragile. They are struggling because they have been strong in the wrong way for too long. They have compensated, masked, overextended, and adapted without acknowledgment or support. That kind of strength looks like competence right up until it collapses. When it does, the collapse is blamed rather than understood.

This book is not an endpoint. It is a reframing. It asks different questions than the profession is used to asking. Not "why did this happen," but "under what conditions did this become likely." Not "who failed," but "what system made failure predictable." Not "how do we punish this," but "what would have prevented it."

Those questions do not weaken the law. They strengthen it.

If the legal profession wants to retain capable, ethical, driven lawyers who happen to have ADHD, it must learn to see them accurately. That means seeing their strengths without romanticizing them and seeing their vulnerabilities without moralizing them. It means accepting that cognition is not uniform and that justice, if it means anything, must account for that reality.

The final truth is simple, even if living it is not. A system that refuses to see clearly will keep repeating the same mistakes and calling them standards. A system that chooses clarity has a chance to evolve.

This book exists because that choice still has not been made often enough.

Whether it will be made next is no longer a question of knowledge. It is a question of will.

www.ingramcontent.com/pod-product-compliance
Lightning Source LLC
Chambersburg PA
CBHW051314130726
47987CB00004B/1807